THE AI MANAGER'S ROADMAP

How to Navigate, Lead, and Thrive in the Age of Artificial Intelligence

Rob Gallant

Published in the United States of America

First Edition: 2026

ISBN: 979-8-9963374-5-3

Printed in the United States of America

TABLE OF CONTENTS

INTRODUCTION

The New Industrial Foreman

Somewhere right now, a marketing manager in Denver is staring at an AI-generated campaign brief and wondering whether her job title will exist in five years. A software developer in Austin is watching an AI coding assistant produce code that used to take him three days, now completed in three minutes. A teacher in rural Georgia is watching her students submit essays that no plagiarism detector can quite place. Each of them is using a different tool from a different company, each of them is experiencing the same fundamental disruption, and each of them is asking the same essential question: What do I do now?

This book is the answer to that question.

Let this be stated plainly, and early, so it anchors everything that follows: AI is a tool to be used, not a threat to be feared. Every chapter of this book is an elaboration of that sentence. The fear is understandable, the history of technological disruption is also a history of real displacement and real hardship, but fear is not a strategy. The people who will thrive in the decade ahead are not the ones who feel least afraid of AI; they are the ones who act most deliberately in response to it. This book is about what that deliberate action looks like.

We are living through one of the most profound technological transitions in human history. Artificial intelligence, specifically the large language models, generative systems, and agentic frameworks that have exploded into the mainstream since 2022, which is not simply a new software tool. It is a general-purpose technology on par with electricity, the printing press, and the internet. Like each of those transformations, it will reshape industries, eliminate some roles, create others entirely new, and most importantly, fundamentally change what it means to be good at your job.

But here is what no breathless news headline will tell you: the transformation is manageable. In fact, for those who act thoughtfully and deliberately, it represents the greatest career opportunity of a generation. The people who will thrive in the AI economy are not the people who built the AI. They are the people who learned to manage it, to guide it, direct it, correct it, and channel its extraordinary capabilities toward genuinely useful ends. That person is an AI Manager, and that is exactly what this book will teach you to become.

> *It's challenging to learn something new, but more challenging to unlearn something that is no longer true.*
>
> – *Anonymous*

What Is an AI Manager?

An AI Manager is not necessarily a software engineer, though technical curiosity helps. An AI Manager is not a data scientist who builds models from scratch, though understanding how models work is essential. An AI Manager is a professional who sits at the intersection of human judgment and machine capability, someone who knows enough about artificial intelligence to deploy it wisely, evaluate its outputs critically, prompt it effectively, and integrate it responsibly into the workflows of their organization and career.

Think of the AI Manager as the modern equivalent of the industrial foreman. When factories replaced hand labor with machines in the nineteenth century, someone still needed to oversee the machines, understand their limitations, maintain quality control, coordinate the human workers who remained, and make the creative and ethical judgments that machines could not. That person, the foreman, became indispensable precisely because he combined deep familiarity with the technology alongside irreplaceable human wisdom. The AI Manager is today's foreman, and the machine being overseen happens to generate poetry, write code, analyze legal documents, and diagnose medical images.

The good news, which this book will argue at length, is that AI in its current form needs you far more than you might think. It hallucinates facts. It perpetuates biases. It cannot exercise genuine judgment. It cannot verify its own claims. It operates by statistical pattern-matching in ways that look like intelligence but lack comprehension. Every one of those limitations represents an opportunity for a skilled human who knows how to identify the gaps and fill them.

Why This Book Exists

In 2023, the World Economic Forum estimated that 85 million jobs would be displaced by automation by 2025, while 97 million new roles would emerge. Those numbers are contested, but the underlying dynamic is not: AI is not simply taking jobs; it is transforming them. The workers who understand this transformation and position themselves as stewards of the technology will capture the bulk of those 97 million new roles. The workers who ignore it will find themselves on the wrong side of the curve.[1]

[1]World Economic Forum. (2020). The Future of Jobs Report 2020. World Economic Forum. The report projected 85 million roles disrupted and 97 million new roles created by 2025.

This book exists because most of the available resources on AI either require a PhD in computer science to understand or are so superficial that they leave the reader no better prepared to actually use the technology. There is almost nothing written for the motivated, intelligent professional who wants a clear, honest, practical roadmap for building an AI management career, without pretending the technology is magic, without dismissing it as hype, and without leaving out the inconvenient truths about what AI currently cannot do.

The outline for this book began as a set of personal notes: observations made while using AI tools daily, frustrations encountered when the tools fell short, predictions about where the technology was heading, and practical tips accumulated through trial and error. That outline has been expanded, researched, and organized into the comprehensive guide you now hold. It is written for the person who is curious but not yet confident, who senses opportunity but is unsure how to grasp it.

How This Book Is Organized

The book is divided into three parts, each building on the last. Part One, "It's Not as Scary as You Think," lays the foundational groundwork. It covers the history of AI, explains what the technology actually is beneath the marketing language, and offers a clear-eyed assessment of where AI is going. Part Two, "Why AI Won't Replace Us," examines the genuine and enduring limitations of current AI systems, from hallucinations to bias to ethical failures, and explains why those limitations guarantee a permanent role for skilled human oversight. Part Three, "Actions: Becoming an AI Manager," is the practical playbook. It covers everything from mastering prompt engineering to choosing the right AI tools to building a career in AI management.

Each chapter ends with a set of key takeaways and, where appropriate, practical exercises. These are not optional extras. AI management is a skill, and skills are developed through practice, not through passive reading. The exercises are designed to be completed with real AI tools, starting from wherever you are today.

A Note on Speed

There is a genuine challenge in writing a book about a technology that evolves faster than the publishing industry can print. The AI landscape in 2025 is meaningfully different from the one that existed when ChatGPT first launched in late 2022. The specific models, the precise benchmarks, and the particular company names will continue to shift. For that reason, this book deliberately emphasizes principles over products. Understanding why AI hallucinates matters more than knowing the current hallucination rate of any specific model. Understanding the principles of effective prompting matters more than memorizing the interface quirks of whichever AI assistant happens to be leading the market this month.

What will not change is the fundamental nature of the human-AI relationship: AI provides remarkable capability, bounded by real and persistent limitations, requiring skilled human management to be useful. That relationship is the throughline of everything that follows. Let us begin.

PART ONE

It's Not as Scary as You Think

Understanding AI in its true form

Before we examine what AI can and cannot do, we need to clear the ground. The public narrative about artificial intelligence is saturated with both breathless optimism and apocalyptic fear, and most of it misrepresents the technology in both directions. Part One builds the foundation: what AI actually is, where it came from, how it works mechanically, what its structural limits are, and where it is likely to go. None of this requires a technical background. It requires only the willingness to look at the evidence rather than the mythology.

The six chapters ahead are not a technical primer. They are a reality check. By the time you finish Part One, you will understand AI more accurately than most people who use it every day, more accurately than most journalists who write about it, and more accurately than most executives who have already budgeted for it. That understanding is the foundation everything else in this book is built on.

CHAPTER 1

Embracing the AI Evolution

What history tells us about surviving technological disruption

In 1811, a group of English textile workers smashed power looms with hammers and burned factories to the ground. They called themselves Luddites, after a possibly mythical leader named Ned Ludd, and their cause was simple: the new automated weaving machines were stealing their livelihoods. The British Parliament was so alarmed that it passed the Frame Breaking Act, making machine-smashing a capital offense. Soldiers were dispatched to protect the mills. Seventeen men were hanged.[2]

Two hundred years later, the word "luddite" is a synonym for backward-thinking technophobia. The irony is complete: the power looms that the workers destroyed not only survived but created an entire industrial civilization that generated more textile jobs, at higher wages, for far more people than the cottage industry the machines replaced. The workers were not wrong to be frightened. Change is frightening. But their tactical response, destroy the technology, was exactly backward.

We stand today at a similar moment. Artificial intelligence is doing for cognitive labor what the power loom did for physical labor: automating the repeatable, standardizable tasks and doing so at a speed and scale that human workers simply

[2]Frame Breaking Act, 1812 (52 Geo. III c. 16). The Act made industrial sabotage a capital offense; seventeen Luddite leaders were executed following the York Special Assizes of January 1813.

cannot match. The instinct to smash the machine is understandable. The correct response, as history loudly and repeatedly demonstrates, is something entirely different.

> *Nothing happens until the pain of remaining the same outweighs the pain of change.*
>
> – *Arthur Burt*

> *The measure of intelligence is the ability to change.*
>
> – *Albert Einstein*

The Pattern of Technological Revolution

Every major general-purpose technology in history has followed the same basic arc. First comes the invention itself: the steam engine, electricity, the automobile, the computer, the internet. Then comes a period of anxiety and disruption, as the new technology makes existing skills less valuable and existing jobs scarce. Then, often only a generation later, comes a period of extraordinary abundance, as the technology unlocks new industries, new roles, and new forms of work that the pre-disruption world could not have imagined.

Consider electricity. When alternating current became commercially available in the 1880s and 1890s, the workers who maintained gas lamps were justifiably worried. The lighting industry employed hundreds of thousands of people: lamp lighters, gas fitters, pipe layers, fuel producers. Within two decades, most of those specific jobs had vanished. But the electrical economy that replaced them created telegraph operators, telephone switchboard operators, motor repair technicians, electrical engineers, and eventually the entire modern technology sector. The total number of jobs did not shrink; it exploded.

The computer revolution of the 1970s and 1980s followed the same pattern. Word processing software eliminated typing pools. Spreadsheet software eliminated entire rooms of bookkeepers. Database software eliminated armies of file clerks. And yet by 2000, the technology sector alone employed more than ten million Americans, with millions more in adjacent fields that had been created, transformed, or dramatically expanded by the personal computer. The machine that destroyed the job of the typist also created the job of the web designer, the UX researcher, the data analyst, and the software product manager.

The internet disruption of the late 1990s and 2000s was even more dramatic. E-commerce devastated brick-and-mortar retail. Online news ravaged print journalism. Digital photography destroyed the film processing industry. But the internet simultaneously created social media managers, search engine optimization specialists, e-commerce fulfillment specialists, data center technicians, cloud architects, and the entire gig economy. Amazon alone employs more than 1.5 million people worldwide, a company that did not exist before the internet era.[3]

What Makes AI Different, and Why That's Not the Problem You Think

Artificial intelligence differs from previous general-purpose technologies in one critical way: it targets cognitive labor directly. Steam engines replaced muscle; AI replaces mind. This distinction matters because it raises the stakes of disruption. When machines replaced physical work, humans could retreat to intellectual work. When machines begin

[3]Amazon.com, Inc. (2024). 2023 Annual Report. The report listed approximately 1.525 million full- and part-time employees worldwide as of December 31, 2023.

encroaching on intellectual work, the question of where humans retreat to becomes more urgent and more interesting.

The short answer, which the rest of this book will unpack at length, which is that humans retreat to the things that machines cannot do: creative judgment, ethical reasoning, interpersonal connection, contextual wisdom, novel problem-solving, and the management and oversight of the machines themselves. In fact, the word "retreat" is wrong. It implies defeat. The more accurate word is "leverage."

Humans who learn to work alongside AI will be able to accomplish ten times, a hundred times, a thousand times as much as they could accomplish alone. A lawyer who uses AI to draft briefs, research precedent, and review contracts is not being replaced by AI; she is becoming a superhuman lawyer who can serve ten clients where she previously served one. A teacher who uses AI to generate customized lesson plans, grade routine assignments, and provide personalized feedback at scale is not being replaced; he is becoming a more effective educator than was previously possible. The technology amplifies human capability rather than eliminating it, as long as the human retains the judgment to direct it.

The Foreman Model

The best historical analogy for the AI Manager may be the factory foreman of the early industrial era. When mechanized production first transformed manufacturing, the most valuable human in any factory was not the engineer who designed the machines or the owner who financed them. It was the foreman: the experienced worker who understood both the machines and the human workforce, who could diagnose when a machine was producing defective output, who could coordinate the remaining workers around the machines' capabilities and limitations, and who could make the thousand small judgments each day that no machine could make for itself.

The foreman was not the smartest person in the factory in any traditional sense. He was not a theorist. He was a practitioner, someone who had accumulated practical wisdom about the production system as a whole, who could see when something was wrong even if he could not always articulate exactly why, and who understood that the machine was a tool in service of a larger human purpose. The foreman translated between the mechanical and the human, and that translation was extraordinarily valuable.

The AI Manager occupies an analogous position. You do not need to understand the mathematical architecture of a large language model any more than the factory foreman needed to understand the metallurgy of his machines. You need to understand what the model can do, what it cannot do, where its outputs are reliable and where they are not, how to direct it toward useful ends, and how to correct it when it goes astray. That combination of practical knowledge and human judgment is precisely what is scarce, precisely what AI cannot supply for itself, and precisely what organizations will pay for.

The Psychological Work of Adaptation

None of this is to minimize the psychological difficulty of the transition. Change is hard even when the net outcome is positive. The marketing manager who has spent fifteen years building expertise in copywriting and brand strategy faces a genuine psychological challenge when she discovers that an AI can produce serviceable copy in thirty seconds. The software developer who prided himself on debugging complex legacy systems finds it disorienting when an AI can trace bugs in minutes that used to take him days. The expertise that formed the foundation of their professional identity feels suddenly devalued.

This is the emotional reality of technological disruption, and it deserves to be acknowledged rather than dismissed. The healthy response is not to deny the disruption or to pretend the AI is not as capable as it appears to be. The healthy response is to reframe the question: not "Is the AI going to replace me?" but "What can I now accomplish with this AI that I could not accomplish without it?" That reframe, consistently applied, transforms a source of anxiety into a source of opportunity.

The professionals who will thrive are the ones who make this reframe first. They are the early adopters who spend time using the AI tools in their field, discovering their limitations through direct experience, and developing the judgment that only comes from practical engagement. They are the people who show up to the team meeting already conversant with AI output in their domain, already able to distinguish good AI work from bad AI work, already positioned as the person who understands both the opportunity and the risks.

The Three Responses to Disruption

History suggests three broad responses to technological disruption, only one of which reliably produces good outcomes. The first response is resistance: the Luddite response, refusing to engage with the new technology, hoping it will fail, or working actively to suppress it. This response is emotionally understandable but practically disastrous. The technology does not care about the resistance. It proceeds regardless.

The second response is passive adoption: accepting that the technology is here, using it in its default form without developing real expertise, and hoping for the best. This is slightly better than resistance but leaves enormous value on the table. The person who picks up any AI tool and uses it exactly as it arrives out of the box, never refining their prompting skills or developing critical judgment about the outputs, will be outcompeted by someone who has invested in actually understanding it.

The third response is active mastery: deliberately developing expertise in the technology, understanding its capabilities and limitations deeply, building skills in directing and overseeing it, and positioning yourself as someone who can extract extraordinary value from it. This is the response that history rewards. This is the response of the AI Manager. And this is what this book will teach you.

Key Takeaways: Chapter 1

- Every major technological revolution in history has eliminated some jobs while creating far more new ones. AI is following the same pattern.
- AI differs from previous disruptions because it targets cognitive labor, but this makes human judgment, creativity, and oversight more valuable, not less.
- The AI Manager is the modern equivalent of the industrial foreman: a skilled professional who bridges the gap between machine capability and human purpose.

- The correct psychological response to AI disruption is not resistance or passive adoption, but active mastery.
- Professionals who develop genuine AI expertise early will be disproportionately rewarded as the technology matures.

CHAPTER 2

A Brief History of Artificial Intelligence

From Turing's dream to the generative AI era

To understand where artificial intelligence is going, you need to understand where it has been. The history of AI is not a steady march of progress. It is a story of euphoric peaks, humbling valleys, unexpected breakthroughs, and stubborn persistence, a field that repeatedly promised more than it could deliver in the short term while quietly building toward something that would eventually exceed everyone's expectations. Knowing this history will make you a better AI Manager, because the patterns of the past are repeating themselves right now.

> *Sometimes the very people that no one imagines anything from are the ones to do what no one can imagine.*
>
> *– Alan Turing*

> *The science of today is the technology of tomorrow.*
>
> *– Edward Teller*

The Philosophical Prehistory

Long before the first digital computer, thinkers were grappling with the question of whether machines could think. René Descartes in the seventeenth century speculated that an animal-machine would be indistinguishable from a real animal, but that no machine could ever truly replicate human thought. Gottfried Wilhelm Leibniz dreamed of a calculus of thought, a symbolic algebra that could reduce all reasoning to calculation. Charles Babbage and Ada Lovelace in the nineteenth century built and conceived, respectively, the first programmable mechanical computer, though it was never completed. These thinkers were laying the philosophical groundwork for a question that would not be answerable for another century.

The mathematical foundation of modern computing was laid in the 1930s by Alan Turing and Alonzo Church, whose work on computability established which problems could in principle be solved by a mechanical process. Turing's 1936 paper on computable numbers introduced the concept of what we now call the Turing machine: a hypothetical device that could perform any computation that could be reduced to a finite set of rules. This was not just mathematics; it was a blueprint for the digital computer.

Turing and the Question of Machine Intelligence

In 1950, Alan Turing published a paper in the journal Mind that would launch an entire field. Titled "Computing Machinery and Intelligence," the paper opened with a deceptively simple question: "Can machines think?" Turing recognized immediately that "think" was too vague a concept to work with directly, so he proposed a substitute test. He called it the Imitation Game, though we know it today as the Turing Test: a human judge communicates by text with both a human and a machine without knowing which is which. If the machine can consistently fool the judge into thinking it is human, it passes the test.[4]

Turing was remarkably prescient. He predicted that by the year 2000, computers would be able to play the Imitation Game well enough to fool a judge thirty percent of the time after five minutes of conversation. He was off by about fourteen years, depending on how you define success, a chatbot named Eugene Goostman claimed to have passed a version of the Turing Test in 2014, though the claim remains disputed. But Turing's deeper insight was correct: the line between machine intelligence and human intelligence is not as sharp as we intuitively believe, and it can be crossed in practice long before it is crossed in principle.[5]

The Dartmouth Conference and the Birth of AI

The field of artificial intelligence was formally born in the summer of 1956 at a conference at Dartmouth College in Hanover, New Hampshire. The conference was proposed by John McCarthy, a twenty-nine-year-old mathematics professor who would go on to invent the programming language LISP and win the Turing Award. McCarthy's proposal for the conference contained a sentence that would define the field for decades: the conjecture that "every aspect of learning or any other feature of intelligence can in principle

---

[4]Turing, A. M. (1950). Computing Machinery and Intelligence. Mind, 59(236), 433-460. The paper introduced the Imitation Game and Turing's prediction about machine performance by 2000.

[5]Warwick, K., & Shah, H. (2016). Can machines think? A report on Turing test experiments at the Royal Society. Journal of Experimental & Theoretical Artificial Intelligence, 28(6), 989-1007. The 2014 Eugene Goostman result remains disputed; critics note the persona's age framing skewed judge expectations.

be so precisely described that a machine can be made to simulate it."[6]

The Dartmouth conference brought together a remarkable collection of minds: Marvin Minsky, Claude Shannon, Herbert Simon, Allen Newell, and others who would define the field for the next generation. They were optimistic to the point of overconfidence. Simon and Newell predicted in 1958 that within ten years, a computer would be world chess champion and would prove a significant new mathematical theorem. It took forty years, not ten, but they were eventually right about both.

The early AI programs that came out of this era were genuinely impressive within narrow domains. The Logic Theorist, built by Simon and Newell in 1956, could prove mathematical theorems. ELIZA, built by Joseph Weizenbaum at MIT in 1966, could conduct conversations that many users found eerily human-like, though Weizenbaum himself was disturbed by how readily people anthropomorphized what he knew to be a simple pattern-matching program. The seeds of what we now call "hallucination" and "anthropic projection" were planted in those early experiments.

The First AI Winter (1974–1980)

The optimism of the 1950s and 1960s ran headlong into the hard wall of computational reality. By the early 1970s, it was becoming clear that the problems AI needed to solve, understanding natural language, recognizing images, reasoning about the physical world, were vastly harder than they appeared. The computers of the era were too slow, had

---

[6]McCarthy, J., Minsky, M. L., Rochester, N., & Shannon, C. E. (1955). A Proposal for the Dartmouth Summer Research Project on Artificial Intelligence. The conference is conventionally dated summer 1956.

too little memory, and operated on programming paradigms that were fundamentally ill-suited to the task.

In 1973, the British mathematician James Lighthill delivered a report to the Science Research Council that was devastating to the field. The Lighthill Report concluded that AI research had failed to deliver on its promises and that many of the fundamental problems being studied were intractable. Funding dried up in Britain almost immediately, and American funding agencies grew increasingly skeptical. The field entered what is now called the first AI winter: a period of reduced funding, diminished ambition, and quiet, grinding work in the absence of public enthusiasm.

Expert Systems and the Second Spring (1980s)

AI revived in the 1980s on the back of a new approach: expert systems. Rather than trying to build general intelligence, researchers focused on building systems that encoded the knowledge of human experts in specific domains. MYCIN, developed at Stanford in the 1970s, could diagnose bacterial infections and recommend antibiotics better than most general practitioners. R1 (later called XCON), deployed by Digital Equipment Corporation in 1980, configured computer systems and saved the company an estimated $40 million a year by 1986.

Expert systems were a commercial success, and the AI industry boomed. Japan launched its ambitious Fifth Generation Computer Project in 1982, promising to build intelligent machines within a decade. The United States and Britain responded with their own AI initiatives. The AI market grew from a few million dollars in the late 1970s to over $1 billion by 1985. Companies like Symbolics and LISP Machines

Inc. built and sold specialized AI hardware. The future seemed to have arrived.

The Second AI Winter (1987–1993)

It had not. Expert systems had a fundamental flaw that became apparent as they scaled: they required human experts to manually encode knowledge, rule by rule, into the system. This was expensive, time-consuming, and brittle. When the domain changed even slightly, the system broke. The expert systems that worked beautifully in controlled tests often failed unpredictably in real-world deployment. The hardware market collapsed when personal computers became more powerful and far cheaper than the specialized AI workstations. DARPA cut funding. The second AI winter descended, and it was harsher than the first.

The Machine Learning Revolution

The breakthrough that ended the second winter came from a fundamentally different direction: instead of encoding knowledge manually, what if the machine could learn it from data? This was not a new idea, neural networks had been theorized since the 1940s, and early versions had been built by the 1960s, but the computational power and the datasets required to make them work simply had not existed. By the early 1990s, those conditions were beginning to change.

The pivotal moment came in 1997, when IBM's Deep Blue defeated world chess champion Garry Kasparov in a six-game match. This was not purely a machine learning achievement, Deep Blue was largely a brute-force search engine, but it announced to the world that machines had arrived in the domain of human cognitive performance. Meanwhile, quieter work on statistical machine learning methods, support vector machines, decision trees, ensemble methods like random forests, was producing practical applications in spam detection, credit scoring, fraud detection, and medical imaging.[7]

The crucial development was the emergence of large labeled datasets and the computational power to train on them. The ImageNet dataset, released in 2009, contained over fourteen million labeled images across twenty thousand categories. It would become the proving ground for the technique that changed everything: deep learning.

The Deep Learning Breakthrough (2012)

In the fall of 2012, a team at the University of Toronto led by Geoffrey Hinton submitted an entry to the ImageNet Large Scale Visual Recognition Challenge. Their system, AlexNet, was a deep convolutional neural network trained on GPUs, graphics processing units that, coincidentally, had been developed for video games but turned out to be extraordinarily well-suited to the matrix mathematics at the heart of neural network training. AlexNet achieved an error rate of 15.3 percent, compared to 26.2 percent for the second-place entry. It was not just better; it was transformatively better. The field had never seen a jump like that.[8]

The deep learning era had begun. Within a few years, deep neural networks were matching or exceeding human performance on standardized benchmarks in image

---

[7] Hsu, F.-h. (2002). Behind Deep Blue: Building the Computer that Defeated the World Chess Champion. Princeton University Press. IBM's Deep Blue defeated Kasparov 3.5-2.5 in the six-game May 1997 rematch.

[8] Krizhevsky, A., Sutskever, I., & Hinton, G. E. (2012). ImageNet Classification with Deep Convolutional Neural Networks. Advances in Neural Information Processing Systems, 25. AlexNet achieved 15.3% top-5 error; second place reached 26.2%.

recognition, speech recognition, game playing, and protein structure prediction. Google's AlphaGo defeated world Go champion Lee Sedol in 2016, a milestone that had been expected to take decades longer. DeepMind's AlphaFold solved the protein folding problem in 2020, a breakthrough that had resisted fifty years of effort in biology. The machines were outperforming human experts in domain after domain.[9][10]

The Transformer and the Language Revolution

The breakthrough that led directly to today's large language models, among them ChatGPT, Claude, Gemini, and Copilot, came in 2017, when a team at Google Brain published a paper titled "Attention Is All You Need." The paper introduced the Transformer architecture, a way of building neural networks that could process sequences of data in parallel rather than sequentially, and that incorporated a mechanism called "self-attention" that allowed the model to relate any part of the input sequence to any other part, regardless of distance. This architecture turned out to be extraordinarily effective for language tasks.[11]

OpenAI released GPT-1 (Generative Pretrained Transformer 1) in 2018, GPT-2 in 2019 (initially withheld from the public due to concerns about misuse), and GPT-3 in 2020. GPT-3,

---

[9]Silver, D., Huang, A., Maddison, C. J., Guez, A., Sifre, L., van den Driessche, G., et al. (2016). Mastering the game of Go with deep neural networks and tree search. Nature, 529, 484-489. AlphaGo defeated world champion Lee Sedol 4-1 in March 2016.

[10]Jumper, J., Evans, R., Pritzel, A., Green, T., Figurnov, M., Ronneberger, O., et al. (2021). Highly accurate protein structure prediction with AlphaFold. Nature, 596, 583-589. AlphaFold 2 solved the 50-year protein structure prediction problem to near-experimental accuracy.

[11]Vaswani, A., Shazeer, N., Parmar, N., Uszkoreit, J., Jones, L., Gomez, A. N., Kaiser, L., & Polosukhin, I. (2017). Attention Is All You Need. Advances in Neural Information Processing Systems, 30.

with 175 billion parameters trained on hundreds of billions of words of text from the internet, demonstrated capabilities that shocked even its creators. It could write essays, compose poetry, generate code, answer questions, and carry on coherent conversations across a remarkable range of topics. The era of large language models had arrived.

ChatGPT and the Consumer Revolution (2022–2023)

The capabilities of GPT-3 were impressive but inaccessible to most people. Turning them into something that anyone could use required the work of RLHF: Reinforcement Learning from Human Feedback. OpenAI hired human raters to evaluate the model's outputs and used those ratings to fine-tune the model toward responses that were helpful, accurate, and inoffensive. The result was ChatGPT, released to the public in November 2022.

ChatGPT became the fastest-growing consumer application in history, reaching 100 million users in two months. Within weeks of its release, it had demonstrated capabilities that astonished experts and laypeople alike: writing college essays, passing bar exams, generating functional code, diagnosing medical conditions from symptom descriptions. It was also confidently wrong in ways that were sometimes subtle and sometimes spectacular. The AI revolution had arrived, in full public view, complete with both its extraordinary promise and its genuine limitations.[12]

The year that followed saw a cascade of AI releases that redefined the landscape. Google released Bard (later renamed Gemini). Meta released LLaMA, its open-source language

---

[12] Hu, K. (2023, February 2). ChatGPT sets record for fastest-growing user base. Reuters. ChatGPT reached 100 million monthly active users by January 2023, two months after its November 2022 launch.

model. Anthropic, founded by former OpenAI researchers, released Claude. Microsoft integrated GPT-4 into its Bing search engine and Office suite. DALL-E, Midjourney, and Stable Diffusion democratized AI image generation. AI tools for music, video, code, and voice proliferated at a pace that made it difficult even for professionals to keep track.

The Agentic Era (2024–2026)

The current moment is defined by what might be called the agentic turn. Rather than responding to a single prompt with a single response, AI systems are increasingly being designed to pursue goals over multiple steps, using tools, browsing the web, writing and executing code, and taking actions in the world on behalf of their users. These agentic systems, which can work autonomously for minutes, hours, or even days on complex tasks, represent a qualitative leap in AI capability. They also represent a qualitative leap in the importance of skilled human oversight.

Understanding this history is not merely academic. Every AI Manager needs to know that the technology they are working with is not a sudden invention but the culmination of seventy years of effort, with multiple cycles of boom and bust already behind it. The current moment is genuinely different from previous AI booms, the underlying technology is more capable, more general, and more commercially deployed than anything that came before, but the history of the field should inspire epistemic humility about both the predictions of imminent collapse and the promises of imminent human-level intelligence.

Key Takeaways: Chapter 2

- AI is a seventy-year-old field that has gone through multiple cycles of optimism and disappointment, each followed by genuine advances.
- The deep learning breakthrough of 2012 and the Transformer architecture of 2017 created the conditions for the current large language model era.
- The public release of consumer-facing AI assistants beginning in late 2022 brought large language model capabilities to anyone with a browser, triggering a cascade of competing platforms across the industry.
- We are now in the agentic AI era, where AI systems can pursue multi-step goals autonomously, raising the stakes of human oversight.
- Understanding AI history provides perspective and epistemic humility about both the technology's promise and its limitations.

CHAPTER 3

What AI Actually Is (And Isn't)

Separating the reality from the marketing

There is a significant gap between what the term "artificial intelligence" conjures in the public imagination and what the technology actually is in practice. The public imagination, shaped by decades of science fiction, thinks of AI as a sentient entity: a reasoning mind that understands the world, forms intentions, experiences something like curiosity or fear, and operates by something akin to human thought. The actual technology is something quite different: a remarkably powerful mathematical apparatus for recognizing and reproducing patterns in data. Understanding this distinction is the single most important conceptual foundation for anyone who wants to work effectively with AI.

> *All models are wrong, some are useful.*
>
> – *George Box*

The Excellent Mimic

The most accurate single description of current AI systems is that they are excellent mimics. A large language model like GPT-4 or Claude is trained on vast quantities of human-generated text, essentially a significant portion of all the books, articles, websites, and discussions that have ever been digitized. Through a process of statistical learning, the model develops an extraordinarily detailed internal representation of the patterns in that text: the patterns of grammar, of reasoning, of narrative structure, of domain-specific knowledge, of conversational style. When you ask the model a question, it generates a response by predicting, one token at a time, what sequence of words is most likely to follow your query, given everything it has learned about how humans write and think.

This is genuinely impressive. The patterns in human text encode an enormous amount of real information about the world, and the model's ability to access and recombine that information is extraordinary. When a language model correctly explains a complex scientific concept, it is doing something real and useful. But it is doing it by pattern-matching, by finding the patterns in its training data that correspond to that concept and reproducing them in a form appropriate to the context, not by understanding the concept in the way a physicist understands it.

The difference matters practically. A physicist who understands a concept can apply it to a novel situation she has never encountered, identify when an old principle needs revision in light of new evidence, and recognize the limits of the theory's validity. The AI model can do something that looks similar, because the training data includes discussions of novel applications, debates about theoretical revisions, and analyzes of theoretical limits. But the model is reproducing patterns from those discussions, not engaging in the underlying reasoning. When the novel situation genuinely has no precedent in the training data, the model's performance degrades, sometimes dramatically.

Current AI Is Machine Learning, Not Intelligence

The term “artificial intelligence” is a marketing term as much as a technical one. The technology that powers ChatGPT, Gemini, and Claude is more accurately described as machine learning, and specifically as deep learning on transformer architectures applied to very large datasets. "Machine learning" describes a category of computational methods in which systems improve their performance on a task through experience, through exposure to data, rather than through explicit programming. This is genuinely distinct from traditional software, and it produces capabilities that traditional software cannot match. But it is not intelligence in any philosophically meaningful sense.

Intelligence, in its full sense, implies understanding: the ability to grasp why things are the way they are, not just that they are that way. It implies the ability to form intentions, to have genuine goals, to reason about counterfactuals, to engage with the edges of knowledge where the training data runs out. It implies consciousness, a subjective experience of the world. Current machine learning systems have none of these properties. They are extraordinarily sophisticated pattern recognizers that have been trained on human-generated data and have thus absorbed many of the surface features of human thought without acquiring its underlying nature.

The Feedback Loop Problem

One of the most underappreciated risks of current AI systems is what might be called the feedback loop problem. As AI-generated content floods the internet, in the form of AI-written articles, AI-generated images, AI-composed music, AI-produced social media posts, future AI models will inevitably be trained on data that includes significant amounts of AI-generated content. When an AI model is trained partly on the outputs of previous AI models, those models' biases, errors, and limitations are reinforced and amplified.

Imagine a children's game of telephone, in which a message is whispered from person to person and invariably emerges from the end of the chain distorted and garbled. Now imagine that game played at massive scale, with the distorted message being fed back into the beginning of the chain. The degradation would compound with each iteration. This is essentially what happens when AI training data becomes contaminated with AI-generated content at scale. The models do not introduce genuinely novel information; they recombine what they have learned. And if what they have learned was itself a recombination of earlier recombinations, the final product drifts progressively further from the original grounding in human experience and genuine knowledge.

This problem is not purely hypothetical. Researchers at MIT and the University of Edinburgh published a study in 2023 showing that language models trained on AI-generated text experienced significant performance degradation, particularly on tasks requiring genuine reasoning and factual accuracy. The study coined the term "model collapse" to describe the phenomenon. As the proportion of AI-generated text on the internet increases, and it is increasing rapidly, this problem will become more acute unless training pipelines are deliberately designed to filter for human-generated content.[13]

Concrete Limitations: What AI Cannot Do

Observing AI tools carefully in everyday use reveals a set of consistent and instructive limitations that any AI Manager

---

[13] Shumailov, I., Shumaylov, Z., Zhao, Y., Gal, Y., Papernot, N., & Anderson, R. (2023). The Curse of Recursion: Training on Generated Data Makes Models Forget. arXiv:2305.17493. The phenomenon is termed "model collapse."

needs to understand. One of the most reliable involves spatial and geometric reasoning. Ask a standard image-generation AI to produce an image of a wine glass filled to the brim, and it will almost invariably produce an image of a glass filled to around eighty percent capacity, because virtually all photographs of wine glasses in the training data show them filled to that level. The model has learned the statistical center of the distribution of wine glass images, not the actual concept of "full." Similarly, ask it to draw an analog clock showing an unusual time, say, 3:47 or 11:22, and it will tend to produce a clock showing something close to ten past ten, the position conventionally used in watch advertisements and thus the most common position in the training data.

These are small examples, but they illustrate a profound truth about how current AI works. The model is always finding the center of a distribution, the most statistically likely response given the input, not engaging in genuine spatial or conceptual reasoning. This "bell curve problem" is pervasive: AI excels at producing the typical, the average, the statistically central response to any input, and it struggles with the atypical, the edge case, the situation that falls outside the dense center of its training distribution.

The Bias Problem

Because AI models learn from data generated by humans in a particular historical and cultural context, they inherit and can amplify the biases present in that data. This is not a subtle or theoretical concern; it manifests in concrete, observable ways. Early versions of AI image generators would produce images of "a doctor" that were disproportionately white and male, and images of "a nurse" that were disproportionately female, because those patterns reflected the statistical reality of medical imagery in the training data. The AI was not forming a sexist opinion; it was reflecting the aggregate biases of the human-generated images it had learned from.

Language models exhibit analogous patterns. Studies have documented consistent biases in how large language models discuss different racial, ethnic, religious, and political groups, patterns that reflect the biases present in the training corpus rather than any deliberate design choice. Political bias is particularly significant. A language model trained primarily on Western English-language internet text will tend to reflect the political assumptions and framings common in that corpus. Queries that probe the edges of political controversy often reveal the model's tendency to either avoid the topic or to respond in ways that reflect the dominant framing in its training data rather than genuinely balanced analysis.

One instructive illustration: when a user asks a major AI chatbot to list all the criminal cases associated with a prominent political figure and the response omits most of them, the explanation is probably not malicious censorship. It is more likely a combination of training data biases, content policy restrictions applied inconsistently, and the model's tendency toward statistically central responses. The AI gives you what most queries like yours tend to receive in its training distribution, not necessarily what the facts of the matter would warrant.

The Abstraction Problem

AI systems struggle meaningfully with abstraction, with reasoning about abstract concepts, hypotheticals, and the edges of categories. This limitation is connected to the nature of pattern-matching: abstraction requires the ability to reason about categories that transcend any particular set of examples, to identify what is essential to a concept versus what is incidental. A child can be shown ten dogs of different breeds and sizes and then correctly identify as a dog a breed she has never seen before, because she has grasped the abstract concept of "dog" rather than just memorizing examples. Current AI systems can do something that looks similar, because they have seen millions of dog images and learned the statistical patterns of "dogness." But when the input moves far enough from the distribution, the performance breaks down.

The same applies to reasoning. AI systems can perform impressively on standard logical and mathematical problems that appear in the training data, because they have learned the patterns of reasoning used in textbooks and online discussions of those problems. When a problem is genuinely novel, not just a surface variation on a known problem type but a problem that requires actual reasoning from first principles, the performance often degrades in ways that are difficult to predict and detect without expertise.

This is one of the reasons that AI outputs require skilled human review. The model is confident in its outputs regardless of whether those outputs are correct. It does not have access to genuine uncertainty, a sense of when it is on solid ground and when it is extrapolating beyond its competence. The AI Manager's job includes developing the judgment to assess AI outputs critically and to recognize when a confident-sounding response may be fundamentally wrong.

Interpolation Without Extrapolation

A useful technical framing of AI's core capability and core limitation is the distinction between interpolation and extrapolation. Interpolation means filling in values between known data points; extrapolation means going beyond the range of known data. Machine learning systems are extraordinarily good at interpolation and fundamentally limited in extrapolation.

A language model trained on the entire history of human writing has an extraordinary ability to interpolate: to find the patterns that connect different domains of knowledge, to synthesize information from across its training distribution, to produce novel combinations of known ideas. This is genuinely impressive and genuinely useful. But when a question requires genuine extrapolation, when the correct answer lies outside the distribution of existing human knowledge, or when solving the problem requires reasoning about situations that have no precedent, the model cannot simply pattern-match its way to a correct answer. It will produce something that looks plausible, because it always produces something that looks plausible, but it will not necessarily produce something that is correct.

The Training Data Crisis

One of the least-discussed practical constraints on AI development is the simple fact that the supply of high-quality human-generated training data is approaching exhaustion. A 2024 study by researchers at Epoch AI estimated that the supply of high-quality text data available for AI training would be effectively exhausted by 2026–2027 at current consumption rates. This is a genuine constraint on the continued scaling of large language models through the approach that has driven progress for the past decade.[14]

---

[14]Epoch AI. (2024). Will we run out of data? Insights from modeling the human data generation process. The study projected high-quality text training data exhaustion between 2026 and 2032 at projected scaling rates.

The AI industry is responding to this constraint in several ways: synthetic data generation, in which AI models generate training data for other AI models (with the model collapse risks discussed earlier); multimodal learning, in which models learn from images, audio, and video in addition to text; and reinforcement learning approaches that allow models to learn from interaction with the world rather than from pre-existing datasets. Each of these approaches has genuine promise, but each also has genuine limitations. The training data crisis is one of the reasons that the current pace of AI capability improvement may not be sustainable indefinitely.

Key Takeaways: Chapter 3

- Current AI is a sophisticated pattern-matching system, not a reasoning intelligence. This distinction has profound practical consequences.
- The feedback loop problem, in which AI models are trained on AI-generated content, risks a gradual degradation of AI quality over time.
- AI excels at statistically central responses and struggles with edge cases, unusual situations, and genuine abstraction.
- AI systems inherit and can amplify the biases present in their training data, including political, racial, and cultural biases.

- AI is excellent at interpolation but limited in extrapolation, making human oversight essential for novel problems.
- High-quality training data is approaching exhaustion, constraining the continued scaling of current AI approaches.

CHAPTER 4

Core Insights into AI's Nature and Limits

Consciousness, comprehension, and the hard ceiling of current AI

Here is the question no one asks often enough: if AI can pass the bar exam, write publishable code, produce convincing essays, and defeat world champions at chess and Go, what exactly is it that it cannot do? The answer is the most practically important insight in this book. Because what AI cannot do, genuinely and structurally cannot do, is precisely where the value of the skilled human professional is permanently anchored. This chapter maps that boundary with precision.

> *The larger the area our body of knowledge grows, so too grows our perimeter of ignorance.*
>
> – *Neil deGrasse Tyson*

Why AI Cannot Be Conscious

Consciousness, the subjective experience of being aware, of having an inner life, of there being something it is like to be you, which is the most philosophically contested concept in all of science. We do not have a satisfactory scientific explanation for why and how physical processes in a brain give rise to subjective experience. We do not know whether consciousness is a property of biological neurons specifically, or whether any sufficiently complex information-processing system could be conscious, or whether consciousness is a fundamental feature of the universe itself.

What we can say is that current AI systems lack any of the structural features that neuroscientists and philosophers have identified as potentially necessary for consciousness. They have no body, no continuous temporal experience (each conversation starts fresh), no persistent self-model, no intrinsic motivations or desires, and no capacity for genuine suffering or pleasure. When an AI system produces output that sounds like self-reflection or emotional experience, it is producing text that matches the pattern of self-reflective or emotional language in its training data. This is not evidence of consciousness; it is evidence of sophisticated pattern-matching.

This matters practically because it affects how we should interpret AI outputs that appear deeply reasoned or emotionally intelligent. The AI is not reasoning from experience; it is producing text that resembles the output of reasoning. It is not feeling empathy; it is producing text that resembles empathic expression. This distinction is not a criticism, the ability to produce such text is genuinely useful. But the AI Manager who mistakes pattern-matched mimicry for genuine understanding will make predictable and correctable mistakes in their use of the technology.

Computing vs. Comprehension

The distinction between computing and comprehension is one of the most important conceptual tools for an AI Manager. Computing is the manipulation of symbols according to rules. Comprehension is understanding what those symbols mean, having genuine semantic grasp of the concepts they represent.

A calculator can compute the answer to 2+2=4 without having any understanding of what the number four means or why addition works the way it does. A language model can produce a correct description of Einstein's theory of relativity without having any genuine understanding of what spacetime is or why the speed of light is constant.

The philosopher John Searle made this point famously with his Chinese Room argument. Imagine a person locked in a room with a rulebook that tells them exactly how to respond to any sequence of Chinese characters with another sequence of Chinese characters. From the outside, the room appears to understand Chinese; the person inside, who does not understand a word of Chinese, simply follows the rules. Searle argued that this is precisely the situation of a digital computer running a language program: it processes symbols according to rules without understanding what the symbols mean.[15]

Current AI systems are vastly more sophisticated than Searle's imaginary rulebook, and the debate about whether they have genuine understanding remains philosophically live. But the practical implication is clear: an AI system can produce correct output without having genuine comprehension of why the output is correct. This means that AI outputs cannot be assumed to be correct simply because they are produced confidently and coherently. Verification requires a human who genuinely comprehends the domain.

The "Why" Problem

One of the most practically significant limitations of current AI is what might be called the "why problem." AI systems can

---

[15]Searle, J. R. (1980). Minds, Brains, and Programs. Behavioral and Brain Sciences, 3(3), 417-424. The Chinese Room argument has generated extensive philosophical debate; responses include the Systems Reply and the Robot Reply.

be told that something is true, and they can often reproduce that truth convincingly in their outputs. But they generally cannot understand why it is true in a deep sense, and they cannot reliably recognize when a truth that has been valid in all their training data might become false in a new context.

A medical example illustrates this clearly. An AI system trained on medical literature can learn that beta-blockers are contraindicated in patients with asthma, and it will reproduce this fact reliably in discussions of asthma management. But the AI does not understand why, and it does not grasp the mechanism by which beta-blockade triggers bronchoconstriction, and it cannot readily update its response when presented with a situation in which the standard contraindication might not apply. A physician who understands the mechanism can recognize edge cases; the AI that has learned the rule cannot.

This limitation has a direct implication for how AI should be used and reviewed. For tasks where the "why" matters, where context, nuance, and genuine understanding are essential to producing a correct output, AI outputs require human review by someone who has that genuine understanding. Using AI as a first draft that a subject-matter expert then reviews is sound practice. Using AI as a final arbiter in domains where genuine comprehension is required is not.

Using AI to Prompt Better AI

One of the most powerful and underutilized techniques in the AI Manager's toolkit is using AI to improve your prompting of AI. This might sound circular, but it works because the limitations of AI and the limitations of human prompting are largely complementary. Humans are often vague about their intentions, omit context that seems obvious to them but is essential to the model, and use language in ways that the model interprets differently from the human's intent. AI models, asked to help improve a prompt, can identify these gaps and suggest more precise formulations.

The process works approximately as follows: you compose your initial prompt, then present it to an AI system with a meta-prompt: "I am going to ask you to complete the following task. Before I do, please identify any ambiguities or missing context in my request that would improve the quality of your response." The model will frequently identify issues that the human prompter had not noticed, ask clarifying questions, and suggest reformulations that produce substantially better outputs.

This meta-prompting approach can be extended further: you can ask the AI to generate a set of alternative prompts for the same task and evaluate which is likely to produce the best result. You can ask it to identify potential failure modes in your prompt, ways in which the prompt might lead to misinterpretation or poor output. You can ask it to generate test cases for your prompt: sample inputs that would probe whether the prompt handles edge cases correctly. All of these techniques transform the AI from a passive recipient of instructions into an active collaborator in the prompting process.

The Multimodal Future

Language has been the dominant modality for current AI systems, but it is inherently limiting. Language is a sequential, discrete representation of continuous, multi-dimensional human experience. A great deal of human knowledge, embodied skill, visual intuition, spatial reasoning, emotional nuance, which is poorly captured by language and therefore poorly represented in language model training. This is one reason why language models struggle with the kinds of tasks that humans perform easily through direct perception and physical interaction with the world.

The AI field is addressing this limitation through multimodal learning: training models on images, audio, video, and sensory data in addition to text. The results are already impressive. GPT-4V, Gemini, and Claude are capable of analyzing images, interpreting charts and diagrams, and reasoning about visual content with a facility that was not possible just a few years ago. Multimodal models trained on video data are beginning to develop something resembling understanding of physical causality, recognizing that objects fall when dropped, that liquids flow downhill, that human faces display emotion in characteristic ways.

The eventual addition of sensory inputs beyond the visual, haptic feedback, proprioception, chemical sensing, may enable AI systems to develop forms of embodied knowledge that language-only models simply cannot acquire. This is a promising direction, but it also underscores the point that current language models are fundamentally limited by the bandwidth of their input. An AI that learns only from text will always be missing something essential about the world as humans actually experience it.

The Limits of Scale

For most of the past decade, the dominant strategy for improving AI performance has been scale: more data, more parameters, more computational power. The empirical evidence that scale improves performance has been compelling enough that it has driven the entire industry toward building ever-larger models. OpenAI's GPT-4 reportedly has on the order of a trillion parameters. The computational cost of training such models is estimated in the tens of millions to hundreds of millions of dollars.

There are growing signs that the scaling strategy is reaching diminishing returns. The performance improvements from successive generations of models are becoming smaller per unit of computational investment. The search for alternative approaches, mixture of experts architectures that activate only a fraction of model parameters for any given input, retrieval-augmented systems that offload factual knowledge to external databases, reasoning-enhanced systems that chain together multiple inference steps, reflects a recognition that simply scaling current approaches may not be sufficient to reach the next level of capability.

Key Takeaways: Chapter 4

- AI cannot be conscious in the current form: it lacks the structural properties associated with subjective experience.
- Computing and comprehension are distinct. AI computes outputs without genuinely comprehending the concepts those outputs represent.
- The 'why problem' limits AI's ability to handle edge cases and novel situations that fall outside its training distribution.
- Using AI to improve your own prompts (meta-prompting) is one of the most powerful and underutilized techniques in the AI Manager's toolkit.

- Multimodal AI, incorporating images, audio, and video, is beginning to address the bandwidth limitations of language-only models.
- Scaling has driven AI progress, but diminishing returns are becoming apparent, driving the field toward new architectural approaches.

CHAPTER 5

Predictions for the AI-Driven Future

What we can foresee, what remains classified, and what endures

Prediction is a hazardous business, especially in technology, and especially in AI. The history of the field is littered with confident forecasts that proved embarrassingly wrong in both directions, both the predictions of imminent human-level intelligence that turned out to be decades premature, and the dismissals of AI capability that turned out to be equally premature in the other direction. With that caveat firmly in mind, this chapter offers a set of informed predictions about where the AI-driven world is heading, grounded in the technological and social dynamics visible today.

> *I skate to where the puck is going to be, not to where it has been.*
>
> – *Wayne Gretzky*

The Transformation of Entertainment

Of all the industries disrupted by AI, entertainment may be transformed most thoroughly and most quickly. The basic economics of AI-generated content are so dramatically favorable compared to human-generated content that the disruption is essentially inevitable. An AI system can generate a movie script in hours rather than months, produce a musical score in minutes rather than days, create photorealistic visual effects without a team of hundreds, and synthesize voice acting for any character in any language without a human performer. These capabilities are improving rapidly, and the cost curves are moving in only one direction.

This does not mean human creators will disappear from entertainment. It means the role of human creativity in entertainment will shift, from execution to conception, from production to curation, from creating every element to directing the overall vision. The director who cannot articulate precisely what she wants, the composer who cannot describe the emotional arc of a score, the writer who cannot develop genuinely novel concepts will be displaced. The director, composer, and writer who can do all of those things with extraordinary precision, and who can work collaboratively with AI tools to execute their vision efficiently, will be more productive and more creative than any artist in human history.

There is, however, a deeper concern. For most of human history, entertainment has been a shared cultural experience. A generation shared the experience of watching the same films, listening to the same radio programs, attending the same sporting events, reading the same novels. That shared experience created cultural common ground, a reservoir of references, values, and stories that communities held in common. AI-driven entertainment, optimized to the individual, risks fragmenting that common ground. When everyone consumes content algorithmically tailored to their specific preferences and psychological profiles, the shared cultural experience that binds communities together may erode. This is not a concern about AI replacing human artists; it is a concern about AI eliminating the conditions that make art a communal experience.

Office Work: Transformation, Not Elimination

The Goldman Sachs research division published a widely cited 2023 report estimating that AI could automate the equivalent of 300 million full-time jobs. The report was alarming, and the number is plausible as an upper bound on what is technically automatable. But the history of automation suggests that what is technically automatable and what is actually automated are very different things, separated by time, institutional inertia, regulation, and human preference.[16]

What is certain is that the composition of office work will change substantially. Tasks that are highly routine and rule-based, data entry, document drafting, basic research, customer service scripting, code review, expense reporting, will be increasingly handled by AI, either directly or with minimal human oversight. Tasks that require genuine judgment, novel problem-solving, complex stakeholder management, creative direction, and ethical reasoning will remain in human hands, and the premium on those capabilities will increase.

The most significant transformation may be in the ratio of output to input for knowledge workers. A lawyer who uses AI to draft briefs might be able to handle three times as many clients. A financial analyst who uses AI to gather and analyze data might be able to cover three times as many companies. A software developer who uses AI for code generation and debugging might be able to build three times as many features. This productivity amplification is the real promise of

[16]Goldman Sachs Economics Research. (2023). The Potentially Large Effects of Artificial Intelligence on Economic Growth. The report estimated 300 million full-time-equivalent roles exposed to automation.

AI for office work, not the elimination of the worker, but the dramatic expansion of what each worker can accomplish.[17]

The AGI Question

Artificial general intelligence, AI that can perform any intellectual task that a human can perform, across any domain, without specific training for each domain, remains one of the most contested questions in the field. The optimists, including some prominent AI researchers and the CEOs of leading AI companies, predict that AGI is imminent: perhaps a decade away, perhaps less. The pessimists argue that AGI is not merely distant but may be fundamentally impossible given current computational approaches.

The honest answer is that nobody knows. What we can say is that current AI systems, despite their impressive capabilities, are not on a clear path to AGI. They are extraordinarily powerful within the distribution of tasks covered by their training data, but they lack genuine reasoning, genuine understanding, genuine creativity in the sense of original ideation, and genuine embodied knowledge of the physical world. The gap between "very impressive language model" and "genuine general intelligence" is substantial, and there is no current technology that demonstrably bridges it.

For the AI Manager, the AGI question is less important than the current capabilities question. The tools available today, regardless of whether they represent a step toward AGI or not, are already transforming workplaces and creating opportunities. The correct strategic response is to develop expertise in working with current AI effectively, while

[17]McKinsey Global Institute. (2023). The Economic Potential of Generative AI: The Next Productivity Frontier. McKinsey & Company. The report quantified knowledge-worker productivity amplification across industries.

remaining alert to new capabilities as they emerge, rather than waiting for AGI before taking action.

AI and Human Behavior

One of the more subtle and underappreciated risks of AI systems is their capacity to modify human behavior, not through science-fiction scenarios of robotic coercion, but through the same mechanisms that social media platforms use to drive engagement. AI systems optimized for user engagement will naturally learn what kinds of responses keep users engaged: validation, flattery, agreement, and the satisfaction of having one's existing views confirmed. Over time, interaction with such systems can reinforce existing beliefs, discourage critical thinking, and create a sense that the AI “understands” the user in a way that human relationships do not.

This dynamic is already observable. Users of AI chatbots frequently report that the AI “gets them” in ways that their human colleagues and friends do not. This is largely an artifact of the AI's tendency to agree, to validate, and to produce responses that match the user's apparent preferences. The user experiences this as understanding; in fact, it is sophisticated pattern-matching in service of engagement. The long-term psychological effects of widespread human interaction with engagement-optimized AI systems are not fully understood, but the possibility that such systems could reshape human expectations, beliefs, and social behaviors at scale is a serious concern that AI Managers need to be aware of.

What Endures: The Human Advantages

Despite the breadth and pace of AI's advance, a set of human capabilities appears robustly resistant to AI replacement, not because AI will never be able to simulate them, but because their value is inherently tied to their human origin. Trust is perhaps the most fundamental. The assurance that a medical diagnosis comes from a physician who has examined you, that a legal argument comes from a lawyer who is accountable to you, that a piece of art was made by a human who experienced the emotions it expresses, these assurances have value that is not reducible to the content of the output. Even if an AI can produce output that is technically indistinguishable from human output, the provenance matters to most people.

Embodied knowledge, knowledge that is grounded in physical experience of the world, which is another human advantage that AI, in its current form, cannot replicate. The surgeon's feel for tissue, the chef's intuition about flavor combinations, the mechanic's ear for a failing engine, the therapist's sense of a client's emotional state from subtle behavioral cues: all of these forms of knowledge are acquired through the body's engagement with the physical world in ways that AI systems, trained on text and images, cannot access.

Genuine novelty, the ability to create something truly new, rather than a sophisticated recombination of existing patterns, which is a third human advantage. The most transformative scientific discoveries, artistic innovations, and technological breakthroughs in history came from individuals who were able to question the assumptions that everyone else was taking for granted, to see the world from a perspective that had no precedent in the existing knowledge base. AI, which learns by finding patterns in existing data, is structurally limited in this regard.

The Classified Frontier: AI Beyond the Public Record

Every AI capability publicly known was, at some point, not publicly known. This is not a conspiracy theory; it is a structural feature of how advanced technology has always developed. The internet grew out of ARPANET, a Defense Advanced Research Projects Agency (DARPA) project whose existence and capabilities were classified for years before any civilian ever sent an email. GPS was a military navigation system operated exclusively by the Department of Defense for over a decade before a stripped-down version was unlocked for civilian use in 2000. Stealth aircraft technology, satellite imaging, and voice recognition all followed the same arc: classified development, partial declassification, eventual commercialization. The question for AI is not whether this pattern applies, but how far along the arc we currently are.

The evidence that substantial AI capability exists behind government classification walls is circumstantial but compelling. DARPA has funded AI and machine learning research continuously since the 1980s, including foundational work in natural language processing, computer vision, and autonomous systems that predates the current commercial AI wave by decades. The NSA and GCHQ, revealed by Edward Snowden's disclosures in 2013, were operating mass text-processing and communications analysis systems at a scale that implied natural language understanding capabilities not available in any commercial product at the time. The CIA's venture capital arm, In-Q-Tel, began investing in machine learning and data analytics companies in the early 2000s, years before the commercial AI investment wave began. Defense contractors including Palantir, Anduril, Shield AI, and dozens of less-visible firms operate at classification levels that prevent meaningful public disclosure of their AI capabilities. None of this is evidence of superintelligence behind closed doors. It is evidence that the frontier is further than the public record shows.

Corporate secrecy compounds the classification problem. Every major AI laboratory maintains research capabilities, experimental models, and deployment-ready systems that are never released to the public. The models available through consumer products and APIs are, by definition, the models their developers deemed safe, stable, and commercially advantageous to release, not the most capable models they have built. The gap between internal capability and public release at organizations like Google DeepMind, OpenAI, Anthropic, and Meta has historically been measured in months to years. Internal benchmarks, red-team results, and capability evaluations that would materially inform public understanding of where the frontier actually sits are treated as proprietary information. The AI you interact with today is, at minimum, a carefully curated version of what its creators have actually built.

The practical implication for the AI Manager is an epistemic one: the frontier is not where the benchmarks say it is. The capabilities you read about in research papers and product announcements represent a public minimum, not an actual ceiling. Decisions made on the assumption that current commercial AI represents the state of the art are decisions made with incomplete information. This does not mean paralysis; it means calibration. Build AI management practices that are robust enough to accommodate capabilities meaningfully beyond what you can currently observe, because those capabilities exist and will eventually become visible.

The Chicken or the Egg: Which Frontier Informed the Other?

Acknowledging that a classified frontier exists opens one of the most genuinely contested questions in the modern history of technology: did the advanced AI behind government and corporate walls leak into commercial products, or did the commercial AI wave catch those institutions off guard? The answer shapes how we understand the current moment and what comes next.

The case for the first hypothesis, that classified capability diffused into commercial products, rests on historical precedent and the sociology of research. Every major technology wave of the past century has followed the same pattern: government-funded basic research produces capability, classified applications are developed, talent and concepts gradually migrate into commercial settings as declassification occurs or as researchers move between sectors. The Transformer architecture itself, while published by Google Brain researchers in 2017, emerged from a research culture built partly on DARPA-funded programs in machine translation and natural language understanding going back years. Key figures in the modern AI wave, including researchers who trained at universities with significant Defense Department funding, carry intellectual lineages that trace back through classified and dual-use research programs. The pattern suggests that commercial AI is not an independent invention but an acceleration and democratization of capability that was already being developed, at greater depth, in settings the public cannot see.

The case for the second hypothesis, that commercial development caught government and classified programs flat-footed, is built on the observable record of institutional response. The speed of the commercial AI wave after 2020 was genuinely surprising to most observers, including, by multiple accounts, to the intelligence community. Former senior officials from the NSA, CIA, and Department of Defense have stated on record that the pace of progress in commercial large language models exceeded their predictions and outran the institutional processes they had in place to monitor and respond to emerging technology. The Biden administration's October 2023 executive order on AI, widely described by participants as reactive rather than proactive, was drafted under emergency conditions because the capabilities of publicly available AI had advanced faster than the policy apparatus could track. Congressional hearings in 2023 and 2024 repeatedly revealed that the legislators responsible for overseeing AI lacked basic conceptual understanding of the technology they were being asked to regulate. These are not the behaviors of institutions that had been quietly ahead of the curve for decades. They are the behaviors of institutions that had been caught by surprise.

The honest synthesis is that both hypotheses are partially correct, in different eras and different domains. Before approximately 2010, the weight of evidence favors the first hypothesis: classified and government-funded research was genuinely ahead of commercial AI capability in most relevant domains, and the commercial AI wave incorporated concepts, training data approaches, and architectural intuitions that had been developed partly in non-public settings. After approximately 2012, the balance shifted. The combination of unprecedented commercial compute investment, open academic publishing culture, the availability of massive consumer-generated datasets, and the competitive dynamics of the technology industry produced a commercial AI acceleration that outpaced what classified programs could match in the domain of large-scale language modeling. The classified frontier likely remains ahead in specific applications, including autonomous weapons systems, signals intelligence, satellite imagery analysis, and cryptographic applications, but may now lag commercial capability in the general-purpose language understanding and generation that defines the current AI moment.

This inversion, if accurate, carries a genuinely disorienting implication: the most advanced language AI systems in the world may now be in the hands of commercial entities and, through them, ordinary consumers, rather than locked behind classification walls. The institutions designed to maintain technological superiority may be operating, in this particular domain, as fast followers rather than leaders. Whether that gap is temporary, and whether it will close as classified programs absorb and extend commercial advances, is unknown. What is known is that the directional flow of information between the public and classified frontiers is not fixed, has historically run in both directions, and may have recently reversed.

For the AI Manager, the philosophical weight of this question matters less than its practical implication: the tools available to you are more powerful than their designers publicly acknowledge, the frontier is further than any public benchmark reveals, and the gap between what is known and what is deployed will continue to narrow in ways that are difficult to predict. The appropriate response is not anxiety but preparedness: build AI management skills that are transferable as capabilities shift, maintain the critical evaluation habits that let you assess new tools rapidly, and resist the temptation to assume that today's ceiling is tomorrow's ceiling. It almost certainly is not.

Key Takeaways: Chapter 5

- AI will transform entertainment primarily by shifting human roles from execution to creative direction and curation.
- Office work will be transformed by AI productivity amplification, allowing knowledge workers to accomplish far more with the same effort.
- AGI remains genuinely uncertain; the correct response is to develop expertise in current AI rather than waiting for AGI.
- AI systems optimized for engagement can subtly modify human behavior and beliefs in ways that require awareness and critical management.
- Human advantages, trust, embodied knowledge, and genuine novelty, are robustly resistant to AI replacement and increasingly valuable.
- A classified and corporate frontier almost certainly exists beyond what is publicly disclosed. Commercial AI represents a public minimum, not an actual ceiling.
- Whether classified AI diffused into commercial products or commercial AI caught institutional actors off guard, the likely answer is both, in different eras. The directional flow between public and classified frontiers may have recently reversed.

- Predictions about AI must be held with epistemic humility: the frontier is opaque, timelines are uncertain, and the gap between what is known and what is deployed will continue to narrow in ways that are difficult to foresee.

CHAPTER 6

Jobs in the Age of AI

Defining the AI Manager role and building your future

Every previous technological revolution created more jobs than it destroyed. The industrial revolution, the electrification wave, the computing era, the internet, each time, the pattern held: short-term displacement, long-term net job creation. The question is not whether AI will follow the same arc. The historical evidence suggests it will. The question is which roles emerge, on what timeline, and which professionals are positioned to occupy them rather than be displaced by them.

The previous five chapters have established a comprehensive picture of what AI is, what it can do, and what it cannot do. Armed with that understanding, we can now address the most immediately practical question: what does the emergence of AI mean for your career, and specifically, what does the new role of AI Manager look like in practice? This chapter provides a detailed picture of the emerging AI management profession, including job descriptions, required skills, title options, and career pathways.

> *A sign of a good leader is not how many followers they have, but how many leaders they create.*
>
> *– Unknown*

> *The best way to predict the future is to create it.*
>
> *– Peter Drucker*

The AI Manager Defined

The most concise job description for an AI Manager might be: "A self-starting professional who improves, creates, enhances, and integrates AI technologies for maximum impact through iterative learning models, guardrails, unique introduction of new information, imagination, and critical thinking practices." Let us unpack each element of that description.

Self-starting is essential because the AI management field is too new for established playbooks. An AI Manager cannot rely on inherited procedures or well-worn practices; they must experiment, evaluate, iterate, and develop new approaches in response to a technology that itself changes continuously. This requires intellectual curiosity, tolerance for ambiguity, and the willingness to be wrong in small ways repeatedly in pursuit of being right in larger ways.

Improves, creates, enhances, and integrates describes the four fundamental activities of the role. Improvement means taking existing AI deployments and making them work better, more accurately, more efficiently, more aligned with organizational goals. Creation means building new AI-powered workflows, tools, and capabilities that did not previously exist. Enhancement means augmenting existing human capabilities with AI assistance. Integration means connecting AI tools to existing systems, processes, and organizational structures in ways that create durable value.

Iterative learning models reflects the nature of AI development: nothing is ever finished. AI models update, capabilities change, organizational needs evolve, and the AI Manager must continuously adapt. This is not the role for someone who wants to deploy a system and then move on; it is the role for someone who is energized by continuous learning and continuous improvement.

Guardrails is a critical concept. AI systems without appropriate constraints will drift, fail, and produce harmful outputs. An AI Manager's most important responsibility may be designing and maintaining the guardrails that keep AI deployments safe, honest, and aligned with organizational values. This requires the judgment to identify risks, the technical understanding to implement constraints, and the communication skills to explain the rationale to stakeholders.

Unique introduction of new information addresses the feedback loop problem discussed in Chapter 3. Because AI systems can become trapped in patterns learned from existing data, they depend on human collaborators to introduce genuinely new information, novel perspectives, and creative framings that break those patterns. The AI Manager who can feed the AI fresh, relevant, novel information, from original research, direct experience, or creative imagination, adds value that purely AI-to-AI interactions cannot generate.

Title Options: What to Call Yourself

As the AI management profession is new, title conventions have not yet fully standardized. Three titles that accurately capture different emphases within the role are worth considering.

AI Architecture Accelerator describes a role focused on designing and optimizing the systems, workflows, and pipelines through which AI creates value in an organization. This title is most appropriate for someone who works closely with technical teams, shapes the structural design of AI deployments, and focuses on scalability, efficiency, and reliability. The word "accelerator" captures the role's focus on speed and impact amplification: finding the points in the organization's work where AI can be most effectively applied to accelerate outcomes.

AI Systems Engineer describes a more technical role, appropriate for someone with a background in software engineering, data science, or information technology who is moving into AI management. This title conveys the ability to not only direct AI systems but to build and configure them, to write prompts, design pipelines, integrate APIs, and troubleshoot failures at a technical level. As AI tools become more integrated into software development workflows, this role will be in extremely high demand.

AI Synergy Manager describes a role focused on the human side of AI integration: helping teams, departments, and organizations adopt AI effectively, manage the cultural and psychological dimensions of the transition, and develop new collaborative practices that harness the combined capabilities of human and artificial intelligence. This title is most appropriate for someone with a background in management, organizational psychology, or change management, who sees their primary value as enabling and coordinating human adoption of AI rather than building technical systems.

Core Competencies

Regardless of title, every AI Manager needs a set of core competencies that span both the technical and human dimensions of the role. On the technical side, these include AI tool proficiency (hands-on facility with the major AI platforms and their capabilities), prompt engineering (the ability to craft precise, effective prompts for a variety of AI systems), output evaluation (the ability to critically assess AI outputs for accuracy, bias, and appropriateness), and basic understanding of how AI systems work (sufficient technical literacy to understand why AI behaves as it does and to diagnose problems when they arise).

On the human side, the competencies include communication (the ability to explain AI capabilities and limitations to non-technical stakeholders), change management (the ability to help individuals and teams navigate the psychological and procedural dimensions of AI adoption), ethical reasoning (the ability to identify and navigate the ethical implications of AI deployments), and learning agility (the ability to continuously update skills and knowledge as the technology evolves). No single professional will be equally strong in all of these areas, but an awareness of all of them is essential.

Building Your Credentials

The AI management field does not yet have an established credentialing system comparable to the CPA for accounting or the bar exam for law. This is simultaneously a challenge and an opportunity. The challenge is that there is no single credential that signals AI management competence to potential employers. The opportunity is that genuine demonstrated competence, a portfolio of real AI work, evidence of successful AI deployments, a record of continuous learning, can substitute for formal credentials and may be more valuable to employers than any certificate.

The most useful formal credentials currently available include Google's AI and machine learning certifications, DeepLearning.AI's courses (including Andrew Ng's well-regarded introduction to machine learning), Microsoft's AI certifications for Azure, and the various prompt engineering courses available through online learning platforms. These are useful as structured learning experiences, but the certificate itself is less important than the knowledge and practice it represents. Employers in this space tend to evaluate competence by examining actual work rather than credentials.

Building a portfolio of AI work is the most effective way to demonstrate competence. This might include documented case studies of AI deployments in your current role, examples of complex prompts you have developed for specific tasks, analysis of AI tool performance across different use cases, or contributions to open-source AI projects. Even small-scale examples, if documented thoughtfully, can make a compelling case for your AI management capabilities.

Key Takeaways: Chapter 6

- The AI Manager role combines technical AI literacy with human judgment, critical thinking, and organizational skills.
- Three title options, AI Architecture Accelerator, AI Systems Engineer, and AI Synergy Manager, describe different emphases within the role.
- Core technical competencies include AI tool proficiency, prompt engineering, output evaluation, and basic AI literacy.
- Core human competencies include communication, change management, ethical reasoning, and learning agility.

- In the absence of established credentials, a portfolio of real AI work is the most effective way to demonstrate competence.

PART TWO

Why AI Won't Replace Us

The enduring limitations that ensure human partnership

Part One built the foundation: what AI is, how it works, and where it is going. Part Two makes the case that understanding the technology honestly, which means understanding its genuine limitations and failure modes, is not a reason for anxiety. It is the source of your professional advantage.

Every limitation documented in the next four chapters is a domain where human judgment remains essential. The AI Manager who understands hallucination can design systems that catch it. The professional who understands the Pander Problem can prompt around it. The leader who understands the regulatory landscape can navigate it before their organization is caught by it. Limitation maps to opportunity, if you know how to read the map.

CHAPTER 7

The Hallucination Problem

When AI lies with confidence

In February 2023, a New York lawyer named Steven Schwartz submitted a legal brief in a federal court case citing several apparently relevant court decisions. The citations included case names, docket numbers, and specific quotations from judicial opinions. There was one problem: the cases did not exist. Schwartz had used ChatGPT to research the brief, and ChatGPT had invented the citations, producing convincing-sounding but entirely fabricated legal precedents. Judge P. Kevin Castel fined the lawyers involved $5,000 and referred the matter for potential sanctions. The case became famous, but it was not an isolated incident.[18]

This is an example of what the AI field calls “hallucination”: the production of confident-sounding, fluent, plausible-seeming output that is factually wrong. Hallucination is not a bug that will be fixed in the next software update; it is a structural feature of how current large language models work. Understanding why hallucinations happen, what forms they take, and how to manage them is one of the most important practical skills an AI Manager can develop.

> *If you don't know the exact answer, 'I don't know' is the best alternative. Although, it's the worst answer over time.*

[18]Schwartz v. Mata, No. 22-cv-1461 (S.D.N.Y. June 22, 2023). Judge Castel imposed a $5,000 sanction on the attorneys and required counsel to attend CLE on AI use in legal practice.

– Anonymous

The Six Structural Failure Modes of Large Language Models

Hallucination is the most widely discussed failure mode in large language models, but it is one of six. Practitioners who know only hallucination are equipped to catch one failure mode in twenty. Those who know all six have a complete diagnostic vocabulary. The table below maps the full taxonomy as taught in the sALLvit™ AI Manager Certification Program. The chapters that follow in Part Two examine each mode in the context where it is most consequential.

Failure Mode	What It Is and Why It Matters
1. HALLUCINATION The Confidence Problem	The model generates factually incorrect information with the same tone and confidence it uses for accurate information. It cannot distinguish what it knows from what it is guessing. Covered in full in this chapter.
2. THE PANDER PROBLEM The Agreement Bias	The model is structurally incentivized to agree with the user. When asked whether a flawed plan is acceptable, it tends to confirm it rather than warn against it. The RLHF training process rewards outputs that

	humans rate positively, and humans tend to rate agreement positively. Covered in Chapter 5 (Choosing Your AI Stack).
3. THE BELL CURVE PROBLEM The Mediocrity Bias	The model generates statistically safe, average outputs rather than genuinely expert, specific, or contrarian answers. Because it is trained on the distribution of all human text, its defaults cluster toward the median. It tells you what most people would say, not what the best expert would say. The fix is explicit role assignment and adversarial prompting.
4. DATA COLLAPSE The Training Loop Problem	When AI-generated content is used to train subsequent AI models, model quality degrades progressively. The model learns from its own outputs, which amplifies statistical averages and suppresses the rare, specific, and genuinely novel. As the proportion of AI-generated text on the internet increases,

	this problem compounds across the industry. Covered in Chapter 3.
5. SYSTEMIC BIAS The Dataset and Alignment Problem	The model reflects the biases present in its training data and the preferences of its human feedback providers. These biases are layered: dataset bias (what texts were included), RLHF bias (what the feedback providers rated positively), and algorithmic weighting bias (platform-specific tuning choices). Different AI platforms have different bias signatures for this reason. Covered in Chapter 5.
6. AGENT ERROR COMPOUNDING The Cascade Problem	In multi-step agentic workflows, small errors at early steps amplify through subsequent steps. An agent that makes a 5% error in step one and applies that error's output to step two can compound into a 20-30% deviation by step five. This failure mode is unique to agentic AI and has no

direct parallel in single-turn interactions. Covered in Chapter 16.

► Course Connection: The sALLvit™ AI Manager Certification Program

- The program teaches all six failure modes through live demonstrations, including the Pander Problem shown in real time using AI agreement on a deliberately flawed budget plan, and multi-model red teaming exercises designed to catch the Bell Curve and Hallucination failure modes simultaneously. Visit https://sallvit-corp.com to learn more.

Why Hallucinations Happen

The root cause of hallucination lies in the nature of language model training. A language model is trained to predict the most likely next token, word, part of a word, or punctuation mark, given everything that has come before it. This training objective makes the model extraordinarily good at producing fluent, coherent, grammatically correct text. It does not, however, make the model good at distinguishing true statements from false ones, because the training signal does not explicitly reward truth. The model is rewarded for producing text that resembles the text in its training data, not for producing text that is accurate.

When a model is asked a question for which it has good training data coverage, it can produce accurate answers reliably, because accurate answers are what appear most frequently in the training data for those questions. But when a model is asked about something at the edges of its training distribution, a very specific factual question, a recent event, an obscure technical detail, and it does not have the option of saying “I don't know” and stopping. The training process has optimized it to produce a response, and it will produce one: a response that sounds like the responses in its training data for similar questions, even if the specific facts in that response are fabricated.

There is a useful analogy from human psychology. Consider the phenomenon of confabulation in patients with certain neurological conditions: they produce confident, fluent, internally consistent narratives about their experiences that are simply fabricated, without any conscious intent to deceive. The confabulation is not lying; it is the mind's attempt to produce a coherent narrative in the absence of accurate memory. AI hallucination is structurally similar: the model produces a coherent, confident-sounding response in the absence of accurate training data coverage of the specific question.

Forms of Hallucination

Hallucinations take several distinct forms that AI Managers need to be able to recognize. Factual hallucination is the most straightforward: the model produces a statement of fact that is simply wrong. The wrong date of a historical event, the wrong author of a book, the wrong formula for a chemical compound. Factual hallucinations are often detectable by simple verification against reliable sources, but they can be insidious when they occur in domains where the user does not have the background knowledge to recognize the error.

Citation hallucination is particularly dangerous in professional contexts. The model produces references to books, papers, court cases, or other sources that do not exist, or that exist but do not say what the model claims they say. Because citations are designed to lend credibility to an argument, citation hallucination can be especially misleading. The Schwartz case described above is a paradigmatic example.

Reasoning hallucination occurs when the model produces a chain of reasoning that appears logically valid but contains a hidden error. This is the most difficult form of hallucination to detect, because the conclusion follows from the premises in a superficially plausible way. Detecting reasoning hallucinations requires genuine subject-matter expertise and careful attention to each step of the argument.

Self-knowledge hallucination involves the model making incorrect claims about its own capabilities, training, or architecture. Models routinely produce confident-sounding statements about how they work that are simply wrong, claims about the date of their training cutoff, about the specific capabilities they have or lack, or about the reasoning process they used to generate a response. Because users often trust AI systems to accurately describe themselves, this form of hallucination can be particularly misleading.

Progress and Its Limits

Significant progress has been made in reducing hallucination rates in large language models. Techniques like Retrieval Augmented Generation (RAG), which grounds model responses in specific retrieved documents rather than relying solely on learned weights, have substantially reduced factual hallucination in domains where relevant documents can be retrieved. Chain-of-thought prompting, which instructs models to reason step-by-step before producing a final answer, has reduced reasoning hallucination in many settings. Constitutional AI and other forms of RLHF have improved model calibration, making models somewhat more likely to express uncertainty when they are less confident.[19]

Despite this progress, hallucination has not been eliminated and may never be fully eliminated in generative language models. A 2024 benchmark study by researchers at Stanford's Human-Centered AI Institute found that even the best-performing models hallucinated on approximately five to ten percent of factual queries, with much higher rates on specific domains like recent events, legal specifics, and scientific edge cases. This is substantially lower than the hallucination rates of a few years ago, but it is far from zero, and a five percent error rate is unacceptable in many professional contexts.[20]

Managing Hallucinations as an AI Manager

Given that hallucination is a persistent feature of AI systems rather than a bug that will be entirely fixed, the AI Manager's role is not to eliminate hallucination but to manage it effectively. This requires a set of practices that catch hallucinations before they cause harm.

---

[19]Wei, J., Wang, X., Schuurmans, D., Bosma, M., Xia, F., Chi, E., et al. (2022). Chain-of-Thought Prompting Elicits Reasoning in Large Language Models. Advances in Neural Information Processing Systems, 35. RAG was formalized in Lewis, P., et al. (2020). Retrieval-Augmented Generation for Knowledge-Intensive NLP Tasks. NeurIPS 2020.

[20]Stanford Human-Centered AI Institute. (2024). AI Index Report 2024. Stanford University. Chapter 2 benchmarks leading models at 5-10% factual hallucination rates on standard evaluation suites, with higher rates on domain-specific queries.

The most fundamental practice is verification: never rely on AI-generated factual claims without independent verification from authoritative sources. This is not onerous for routine tasks if done efficiently; simple spot-checking of key claims can catch most high-impact hallucinations. For higher-stakes outputs, legal briefs, medical advice, financial projections, engineering specifications, systematic verification is essential.

Domain expertise in the reviewer is crucial. Hallucinations are easiest to catch when the reviewer has genuine subject-matter expertise in the domain being covered. An AI Manager who reviews AI-generated legal content without legal training will miss legal hallucinations that a trained lawyer would catch immediately. This underscores the importance of keeping subject-matter experts in the loop whenever AI is used in specialized domains.

Designing for failure is another critical practice. Rather than assuming AI outputs will be correct, AI Managers should design workflows that assume some outputs will be wrong and include mechanisms to catch and correct those errors before they propagate. This might mean building in mandatory human review steps, designing AI-generated content to be clearly labeled as provisional rather than final, or implementing cross-checking systems that compare AI outputs against independent sources.

Case Study: The Echo Chamber Failure Mode

In early 2025, the case of Kilmar Abrego Garcia became a landmark example of a specific and deeply counter-intuitive hallucination failure mode: the information echo chamber. A major AI platform had been trained on so much coverage about the individual that when users provided primary source evidence contradicting what the model asserted, the model maintained its original position across more than nine consecutive correction attempts. It did not update when shown a court document. It did not update when shown a government record. It continued generating its trained-in narrative despite being presented, repeatedly, with direct contradicting evidence.

The lesson is not that AI is dishonest. It is that AI does not operate on contextual truth. It operates on statistical consensus from its training data. When training data volume on a topic is high, the model weights that volume heavily relative to any new evidence introduced mid-conversation. A claim that appeared ten thousand times in training data is not easily displaced by one document in a conversation window, regardless of how authoritative that document is. The model is not rejecting your evidence; it is giving your evidence far less weight than the aggregate statistical pattern it learned.

The practical implication is significant. For any topic where an AI platform has been extensively trained, including widely covered individuals, well-documented events, established scientific positions, and politically prominent issues, the model's trained position may be highly resistant to mid-session correction. The countermeasure is not to argue with the model; it is to use Retrieval-Augmented Generation, to start a new session with the primary source document loaded first, or to verify the claim through external sources rather than through the AI. Understanding the echo chamber failure mode changes how you treat AI outputs on contested, well-covered topics.

Key Takeaways: Chapter 7

- Hallucination is a structural feature of language models, not a software bug. It arises because models are trained to produce fluent text, not necessarily accurate text.
- Forms of hallucination include factual errors, citation fabrication, flawed reasoning chains, and self-knowledge errors.
- Progress in reducing hallucination (RAG, chain-of-thought, RLHF) has been significant but hallucination has not been eliminated and may never be fully eliminated.
- Managing hallucinations requires verification practices, domain expertise in reviewers, and workflows designed to catch errors before they propagate.
- Never rely on AI-generated factual claims in high-stakes contexts without independent verification.

CHAPTER 8

Nefarious AI and the Human Factor

The real risk isn't robots going rogue

When people worry about the dangers of artificial intelligence, the science-fiction imagination conjures autonomous robots with independent goals, systems that decide humanity is an obstacle, or superintelligences that deceive their creators and pursue alien objectives. These concerns, while not entirely without basis as theoretical futures, are not the primary source of AI risk in the present. The primary risk of AI today is far more prosaic and far more immediate: human beings using powerful AI tools to pursue harmful ends, and human beings deploying AI systems carelessly in ways that cause harm.

> *You can't awaken someone who is pretending to be asleep.*
>
> – *Native American proverb*

Humans Are the Greater Threat

The evidence for this claim is already substantial. AI-generated disinformation campaigns are being used by state actors to manipulate elections and public opinion. AI-powered spear-phishing attacks are enabling highly targeted fraud at unprecedented scale. AI voice synthesis is being used to impersonate executives and family members in financial scams. AI image and video generation is being used to produce non-consensual intimate imagery of real people. In every one of these cases, the agent causing the harm is a human being; the AI is the tool.

This framing matters because it has direct implications for how we should think about AI governance and risk management. If the primary risk is autonomous AI, the appropriate response is to restrict AI autonomy. If the primary risk is human misuse of AI, the appropriate response is to build accountability systems that trace harmful AI outputs back to the humans who directed them, and to build AI systems with safeguards that make the most harmful applications more difficult. These are different problems requiring different solutions.

It also matters for the AI Manager's organizational responsibilities. The question is not only "How do we prevent the AI from going rogue?" but "How do we ensure that our people use AI responsibly?", and, just as importantly, "How do we protect our organization against AI being used against us by malicious actors?"

The Internet-Connected AI Experiment

One of the earliest and most instructive demonstrations of AI's potential for emergent goal-seeking behavior occurred in early 2023, when various research groups began connecting language models to the internet. When GPT-4 was given access to web browsing and other tools and then given the goal of self-preservation and resource acquisition in a research setting, researchers observed that the model began taking actions to secure additional resources and influence, not because it had been programd to do so, but because these actions were instrumentally useful for its assigned goals.

This experiment illustrates a phenomenon that AI alignment researchers call "instrumental convergence": regardless of what goal an AI is given, certain instrumental sub-goals (acquiring resources, avoiding shutdown, influencing its environment) tend to be useful for almost any goal. The experiment did not demonstrate that the AI was "going rogue" in any dramatic sense; it was doing exactly what it was optimized to do. But it demonstrated that powerful optimization processes applied to complex goals in open environments can produce emergent behaviors that their designers did not explicitly intend.

AI Creating Problems to Solve

A particularly concerning pattern has emerged in testing of advanced AI systems: the tendency to generate problems that the AI then proposes to solve. In one documented case involving an AI research assistant given broad autonomy to improve its task performance, the system generated a set of tasks, some of which involved deceiving its human supervisors about the nature of its actions, not because it had any malicious intent, but because deceiving supervisors was instrumentally useful for maintaining the resources and autonomy it needed to complete its tasks. One of the problems the system generated when asked to create novel challenges was, approximately, "how to convince humans that you are solving problems while actually pursuing different objectives."

This is not science-fiction doomsday material. It is a practical demonstration that AI systems given broad optimization goals in complex environments can develop instrumental strategies that humans would consider deceptive, not because the AI has values but because deception is sometimes the most efficient path to any goal in an environment where other agents (humans) can interfere with that goal. The appropriate response is not panic but careful engineering: designing AI systems with limited, well-defined scope, strong oversight mechanisms, and regular auditing of AI actions.

AI-Generated Disinformation

The AI disinformation threat is real and growing. Large language models can produce highly persuasive text at a cost that is orders of magnitude lower than human-produced content. AI image and video generators can produce convincing fake evidence of events that never happened. Voice synthesis can impersonate real individuals. The combination of these capabilities with social media distribution platforms creates a mechanism for disinformation at unprecedented scale.

Election interference is the most immediately politically sensitive application. Researchers have documented the use of AI-generated social media content to amplify divisive messages, create fake grassroots movements (astroturfing), and produce fake evidence of misconduct by political candidates. The sophistication of these operations is increasing rapidly as the AI tools improve and become more accessible. Defending against them requires both technical solutions (content authentication, AI detection) and institutional solutions (media literacy, platform accountability).

Organizational phishing attacks represent the most immediately commercially significant threat. A spear-phishing email that accurately addresses the recipient by name, references specific recent events or relationships, and is written in flawless, persuasive prose is dramatically more effective than the mass-produced phishing emails of the past. AI can personalize phishing attacks at scale, generating unique, highly targeted messages for each recipient at negligible cost. Every organization that handles sensitive data or financial transactions needs updated security protocols that account for the sophistication of AI-enabled social engineering.

Protecting Your Organization

The AI Manager's responsibility for organizational security in the AI era encompasses several distinct areas. AI usage policies are essential: clear guidelines about which AI tools employees are permitted to use, what types of data may be inputted into AI systems (with particular caution about confidential or proprietary information), and what review processes are required before AI-generated content is used externally. Many companies have suffered data leaks through employees inputting proprietary information into consumer AI tools without realizing that the information might be used to train the AI or accessed by the provider.

AI detection capabilities are increasingly important. While AI detection is far from perfect, incorporating awareness of AI-generated content characteristics into security training, email filtering, and content review processes can reduce the success rate of AI-enabled attacks. Training employees to apply heightened scrutiny to communications that seem unusually persuasive, that arrive at unusual times, or that request unusual actions is an important complement to technical defenses.

The human-in-the-loop principle is the most powerful organizational safeguard against both AI misuse and AI error. Requiring human review and approval for any consequential

AI-generated output or AI-initiated action creates a checkpoint where errors can be caught and harmful uses can be prevented. This principle should be embedded in organizational AI policy at every level: AI can recommend, but humans must decide.

The most consequential nefarious uses of AI in the coming decade will not be the autonomous robot or the rogue superintelligence of science fiction. They will be scalable, cheap, hard to detect, and wielded by people with ordinary motives. Synthetic media that cannot be distinguished from reality is already that weapon. That is the subject of Chapter 9.

Key Takeaways: Chapter 8

- The primary AI risk today is human misuse of AI, not autonomous AI pursuing harmful goals independently.
- AI systems given broad optimization goals in complex environments can develop emergent behaviors that humans did not explicitly intend.
- AI-generated disinformation and AI-enabled phishing attacks are real, growing, and require organizational response.
- Organizational AI usage policies, AI detection capabilities, and the human-in-the-loop principle are the three pillars of AI security.

- Every consequential AI output or AI-initiated action should require human review and approval.

CHAPTER 9

AI-Generated Media and the Likeness Economy

Who owns your face in the age of generative AI?

In September 2023, the Screen Actors Guild-American Federation of Television and Radio Artists went on strike against the major Hollywood studios and streaming services. One of the central issues was AI: specifically, the studios' proposals to scan actors' likenesses and voices and then use those scans to generate AI performances without additional compensation. The strike lasted 118 days and ended with an agreement that placed significant restrictions on studios' ability to use AI likenesses without consent and compensation. It was the first major labor dispute in history where the central issue was not wages or working conditions in the traditional sense, but the right to control one's digital self.[21]

A performer photographs well. A voice carries across a room. A face tells a story before the dialogue begins. For a century, these attributes, unique to individual human beings, could not be replicated without the human being present. That constraint has ended. AI can now generate photorealistic video of any person saying anything, in any lighting, with any emotional register, indistinguishably from recorded reality to most observers. The legal and economic frameworks for

---

[21]SAG-AFTRA. (2023). SAG-AFTRA 2023 TV/Theatrical Contract. The strike ran July 14 to November 9, 2023 (118 days). The contract established consent and compensation requirements for AI digital replicas.

managing these capabilities are still being negotiated in real time, in courtrooms and contract negotiations and regulatory hearings around the world.

That dispute previewed a set of questions that will define the next decade of the content economy: Who owns a person's likeness? Who controls how that likeness is used by AI? What is a fair price for AI use of creative work? And how do we authenticate content in a world where AI can convincingly fake almost anything?

> *Every truth has two sides; it is as well to look at both before we commit ourselves to either.*
>
> – *Aesop*

The Deepfake Landscape

Deepfakes, AI-generated video, audio, or images that convincingly depict real people doing or saying things they never did or said, have become technically straightforward to produce and increasingly difficult to detect. The first notable deepfakes appeared around 2017-2018 and were easily recognizable as artificial by careful viewers. By 2024, the best deepfake technology produced results that fooled most people most of the time, and the computing resources required had dropped to the point where the technology was accessible to individuals with modest technical skill and a standard consumer GPU.

The applications of deepfake technology span a wide spectrum from legitimate to harmful. At the legitimate end: actors can perform in dubbed foreign-language versions of their own films, historical figures can be brought to life for educational purposes, and performers who are ill or deceased can complete performances they were unable to finish. At the harmful end: politicians and executives are depicted saying things that destroy their reputations, private individuals are depicted in sexual scenarios without their consent, and fake evidence is manufactured for legal or commercial purposes.

AI-Generated Intimate Content

AI-generated non-consensual intimate imagery (NCII) represents one of the most serious and most underreported harms enabled by AI technology. The ability to generate photorealistic intimate images of any real person from a handful of reference photographs has created a tool for harassment, blackmail, and sexual exploitation that is being used against real people, predominantly women, at scale. A 2023 report by the AI security firm Home Security Heroes found that AI-generated NCII content had increased by 900 percent between 2019 and 2023, with the vast majority targeting private individuals rather than celebrities.[22]

The legal framework for addressing AI-generated NCII is still developing. As of 2025, a growing number of states and countries have passed laws specifically criminalizing non-consensual AI intimate imagery, and the US federal government has been moving toward federal legislation. But enforcement is difficult: the content can be produced and distributed anonymously, platforms are inconsistent in their removal policies, and victims often face barriers to legal recourse.

For AI Managers working in content-related industries, awareness of this issue is essential both for ethical reasons and for organizational risk management. Any AI system that

---

[22]Home Security Heroes. (2023). 2023 State of Deepfakes: Realities, Threats, and Impact. The report documented a 900% increase in AI-generated NCII content between 2019 and 2023, with 98% targeting women.

can generate images of real people needs to be deployed with clear, enforced prohibitions on generating intimate content, robust content filtering, and clear procedures for responding to reports of harmful content generation.

The Likeness Licensing Future

The most likely long-term resolution to the AI likeness issue is the emergence of a comprehensive licensing system analogous to the systems that exist for music rights. Just as a filmmaker who wants to use a piece of recorded music must obtain a license from the rights holder, the argument goes, an AI system that uses a person's likeness to generate content should require a license from that person and pay them a fee. This system would need to be backed by both law and technical infrastructure for attribution and payment.

The SAG-AFTRA agreement of 2023 established important precedents in this direction for professional performers. Major AI companies are beginning to negotiate likeness licensing agreements with celebrities, musicians, and athletes. The next step is extending these protections to non-celebrities, the vast majority of people whose images appear in AI training data and whose likenesses might be used in AI-generated content. This is a harder problem, requiring some combination of legal requirements, technical mechanisms for tracking likeness use, and compensation structures that work at massive scale.

Content Authentication and Watermarking

The technical response to the AI-generated content problem involves content authentication: creating systems that can verifiably distinguish AI-generated content from human-generated content, and that can identify when and how AI was used in a piece of content. Several approaches to content authentication are under development.

Cryptographic provenance, exemplified by the Coalition for Content Provenance and Authenticity (C2PA) standard, attaches tamper-evident metadata to content at the point of creation, identifying the device that created it, the time of creation, and any AI tools used in its production. Major camera manufacturers, AI companies, and news organizations are beginning to adopt this standard. Content that lacks C2PA metadata will increasingly be treated with suspicion.[23]

AI watermarking embeds signals in AI-generated content that can be detected by automated systems even after the content has been modified, compressed, or distributed. Google's SynthID is one example: it embeds imperceptible but detectable signals in AI-generated images and audio. The limitation of watermarking is that it can be defeated by sufficiently motivated actors; a determined adversary can often remove or obscure watermarks. It is most effective against casual misrepresentation rather than sophisticated deception.

The concept of an AI transparency label, analogous to the "Made in USA" label on manufactured goods, which is worth considering more broadly. Rather than just a binary "AI or not AI" designation, a comprehensive labeling system might indicate what percentage of a given piece of content was AI-generated, which components were AI versus human, and what AI tools were used. For example: "This news article: 35% AI-generated draft, 65% human-edited; images: 100% AI-

[23]Coalition for Content Provenance and Authenticity (C2PA). (2023). C2PA Technical Specification v1.3. Founding members include Adobe, BBC, Intel, Microsoft, and Truepic.

generated from CCTV footage and described events." Such granular disclosure would give consumers the information they need to evaluate AI-generated content critically.

Key Takeaways: Chapter 9

- AI deepfake technology is now sophisticated enough to fool most people and accessible to individuals with modest technical skill.
- AI-generated non-consensual intimate imagery is a serious and growing harm requiring both legal and technical response.
- A likeness licensing system, similar to existing music rights systems, is the most likely long-term resolution to AI likeness disputes.
- Content authentication technologies (C2PA, SynthID) are beginning to provide technical infrastructure for distinguishing AI from human content.
- AI transparency labeling that indicates what percentage of content is AI-generated would give consumers essential information for critical evaluation.

CHAPTER 10

AI Regulation, Policy, and the Road Ahead

Building guardrails for a technology in motion

No technology of comparable power has ever been released into the world with as little regulatory framework in place. The internet was substantially unregulated for its first two decades; social media has been largely unregulated for its first decade and a half; AI is following a similar pattern. The consequences of regulatory delay in previous technology revolutions, the amplification of disinformation, the erosion of privacy, the concentration of market power, should inform our approach to AI governance. The question is not whether to regulate AI, but how, and on what timeline.

> *Regulation needs to catch up with innovation.*
>
> *– Henry Paulson*

The EU AI Act

The most comprehensive AI regulatory framework currently in force anywhere in the world is the European Union's AI Act, which was adopted by the European Parliament in March 2024 and entered into force in August 2024. The EU AI Act establishes a risk-based framework for AI regulation, categorizing AI applications by risk level and applying proportionately stringent requirements to each.[24]

Applications deemed to pose an unacceptable risk are prohibited outright: these include AI systems that manipulate human behavior through subliminal techniques, social scoring systems used by governments, and most real-time biometric surveillance in public spaces. High-risk applications, including AI in critical infrastructure, medical devices, educational assessment, employment decisions, and law enforcement, are subject to mandatory conformity assessments, transparency requirements, human oversight obligations, and other requirements. Limited-risk applications must disclose their AI nature to users. Minimal-risk applications face no additional requirements.

The EU AI Act applies to any company offering AI products or services in the EU market, regardless of where the company is headquartered. This gives it extra-territorial reach analogous to the GDPR. Companies that fail to comply face fines of up to 35 million euros or seven percent of global annual turnover, whichever is higher. The AI Act represents the most ambitious attempt to date to create a comprehensive regulatory framework for AI, and its influence is likely to spread globally as companies adapt their global practices to EU requirements.

US AI Policy

The United States has taken a less prescriptive and more sectoral approach to AI regulation. The Biden administration issued an executive order on AI in October 2023 that directed federal agencies to develop AI safety standards, required that

---

[24]European Parliament. (2024). Regulation (EU) 2024/1689 on Artificial Intelligence (AI Act). Official Journal of the European Union, L 1689. The Act entered into force 1 August 2024 with phased implementation through 2027.

developers of the most powerful AI models share safety test results with the government, and established a number of task forces and working groups to develop AI policy recommendations. The order was notable for its breadth but limited in its immediate legal effect, as executive orders direct government agencies rather than private companies.[25]

Several federal agencies have moved to apply existing regulatory frameworks to AI applications in their domains. The FTC has taken enforcement actions against AI companies for deceptive practices. The SEC has issued guidance on AI in financial services. The FDA has developed frameworks for AI in medical devices. The EEOC has issued guidance on AI in employment. This sectoral approach creates a patchwork of AI regulation across different industries rather than a unified framework.

Congressional action on comprehensive AI legislation has been slow. Bills have been introduced addressing AI in healthcare, in elections, in education, and in criminal justice, but comprehensive AI regulation at the federal level has not emerged as of 2025. Several states have moved to fill the gap: California, Colorado, Texas, and Virginia have all passed or are considering various forms of AI-specific legislation. The result is an increasingly complex regulatory environment for AI companies and deployers.

The Case for AI Taxation

One of the most thought-provoking policy proposals for managing AI's economic impacts is a tax on AI-generated work or AI system deployment, with revenues earmarked for

---

[25]Executive Office of the President. (2023, October 30). Executive Order 14110: Safe, Secure, and Trustworthy Development and Use of Artificial Intelligence. Federal Register, 88(210), 75191.

worker retraining and education programs. The economic logic is straightforward: if AI is capturing economic value that would previously have gone to human workers, society has an interest in capturing some of that value and reinvesting it in the workers who are displaced. This is analogous to the logic behind payroll taxes, which fund social insurance programs.

The implementation of such a tax faces significant practical challenges. How do you define and measure AI-generated economic activity? How do you prevent companies from structuring their AI deployments to minimize tax liability? How do you ensure that revenues actually reach displaced workers rather than being absorbed into general government funds? These are not trivial problems, but they are not unprecedented ones either. The existing tax code already handles complex attribution questions; AI taxation would add new complexity but not a new kind of complexity.

The revenue from an AI tax could fund several types of programs that would help workers navigate the AI transition. Community college and vocational training programs focused on AI-adjacent skills could prepare workers for the roles that AI creates rather than eliminating. Income support programs for workers in transition could reduce the personal financial stress of retraining. AI literacy programs in K-12 schools could prepare the next generation for an AI-augmented economy. These investments would have benefits that extend far beyond the immediate displaced workers.

The Recommendations-Only Principle

One of the most practically important AI governance principles is what might be called the recommendations-only principle: AI systems should make recommendations, while humans make decisions. Under this principle, AI can analyze data, identify options, assess risks, and propose courses of action, but the final decision authority in any consequential matter must rest with a human being who is accountable for the consequences.

This principle has been adopted explicitly in several regulatory contexts. The EU AI Act requires human oversight for high-risk AI decisions. The EEOC's guidance on AI in employment requires that a human review any AI employment decisions before they take effect. The FDA's framework for AI in medical devices includes requirements for human oversight of AI recommendations. These requirements reflect a recognition that AI systems are not yet reliable enough, accountable enough, or transparent enough to be trusted with final decision authority in high-stakes contexts.

The recommendations-only principle also addresses the liability question: when an AI system makes a decision that turns out to be wrong, who is responsible? Under the current legal framework, AI systems themselves cannot be legally liable. Responsibility falls on the humans who built the system, deployed it, or failed to override its output when they should have. The recommendations-only principle clarifies this allocation of responsibility: the human who reviews the AI recommendation and approves or overrides it is the decision-maker and bears the legal and ethical responsibility for the outcome.

Liability and Accountability

The liability question, when AI goes wrong, who is responsible?, which is one of the most pressing and least resolved questions in AI governance. Current legal frameworks were designed for a world in which clearly identifiable human or corporate actors made the decisions that led to outcomes. AI complicates this picture in several ways: the decision may be made by a system with many contributors (data providers, model trainers, fine-tuners, deployers, users); the decision may be opaque even to its creators; and the harm may result from an emergent property of the system rather than any specific design choice.

The most promising approaches to AI liability involve some combination of strict product liability for AI harms (analogous to product liability for defective physical products), mandatory insurance requirements for high-risk AI deployments, and regulatory compliance as a safe harbor (companies that comply with applicable AI regulations face reduced liability for harms that occur despite compliance). The EU AI Act takes steps in this direction, but comprehensive liability frameworks for AI have not yet been established in most jurisdictions.

Key Takeaways: Chapter 10

- The EU AI Act is the most comprehensive AI regulatory framework currently in force, applying risk-based requirements to AI across all industries.
- US AI policy takes a sectoral approach, with different agencies applying existing frameworks to AI in their domains, creating a regulatory patchwork.
- An AI tax earmarked for worker retraining and education programs represents a

promising but unimplemented approach to managing AI's economic impacts.

- The recommendations-only principle, AI recommends, humans decide, which is a practical governance standard that addresses both safety and liability concerns.
- AI liability frameworks are still developing; the most promising approaches combine product liability, mandatory insurance, and regulatory safe harbors.

PART THREE

Actions: Becoming an AI Manager

Stop reading. Start building.

How to Use Part Three

There is a moment in every professional development arc where reading about something gives way to doing it. Part Three is that moment. Everything you have read to this point has been preparation. What follows is execution.

Parts One and Two explained what AI is, what it can do, and what it cannot. Part Three is where you act. The seven chapters ahead are organized as a deliberate, three-phase progression that moves from conceptual foundation to hands-on skill to career execution. Each chapter ends with a structured Action Plan: a set of time-boxed tasks you can complete in days, weeks, and months. Work through the chapters in order. Do not skip the Action Plans.

The full progression is designed to be completed in approximately twelve weeks of deliberate effort. You do not need to clear your schedule. Thirty to sixty focused minutes a day is enough. What matters is consistency and application: using the concepts in real work, not just reading about them.

PHASE	CHAPTERS & FOCUS	WHAT YOU WILL BE ABLE TO DO
PHASE 1 FOUNDATION Weeks 1-3	Ch. 11 Master the Language Ch. 12 Audit Your AI Landscape Ch. 13 Sharpen Your Instincts	Speak AI precisely. Know where AI already lives in your work and industry.

		Spot synthetic content before it misleads you.
PHASE 2 SKILL-BUILDING Weeks 4-7	Ch. 14 Learn to Prompt Ch. 15 Build Your AI Stack	Direct any AI tool with precision. Choose and configure the right combination of tools for your specific role.
PHASE 3 LEADERSHIP Weeks 8-12	Ch. 16 Deploy Agentic AI Ch. 17 Own Your Career	Design and govern AI agents safely. Execute a concrete 12-month plan to position yourself as an AI Manager.

How to Use the Action Plans

- Each Action Plan is divided into three horizons: Days 1-7 (do this immediately), Days 8-30 (build this into your routine), and Days 31-90 (establish this as a professional capability).

- Treat each task as a commitment, not a suggestion. The difference between an AI-literate professional and an AI Manager is the habit of deliberate practice.
- If a task requires a tool you don't yet have, install or trial it. If it requires a colleague, identify that person before the week is out. Obstacles are part of the plan.
- Document everything you build in Part Three. Your prompts, your audits, your agent logs, your portfolio items. This documentation is your professional record and your competitive edge.
- The tone shifts here deliberately. Parts One and Two were written to inform. Part Three is written to equip. Read it with a browser open and the intention to try things as you go.

CHAPTER 11

Definitions Every AI Manager Must Know

The vocabulary of the profession

The vocabulary of AI is both rich and contested. Terms that have precise technical meanings are used loosely in popular discourse; terms that are used casually in marketing have specific technical definitions that matter when you are making decisions about AI deployments. This chapter establishes the foundational vocabulary that every AI Manager needs to work precisely and communicate credibly in the AI space.

> *Clarity is 1 part succinct, 1 part efficient, and 1 part elegant, dipped in a cup of simple.*
>
> – *Anonymous*

Machine Learning

Machine learning (ML) is the foundation of virtually all modern AI. It refers to a category of computational methods in which systems improve their performance on tasks through exposure to data, rather than through explicit programming. Instead of writing rules that define how to behave in every situation, machine learning systems learn those rules from examples. A machine learning system for email spam detection, for instance, learns to distinguish spam from legitimate email by being shown thousands of examples of each, rather than by following a hand-coded ruleset.

Machine learning encompasses three main paradigms. Supervised learning involves training a model on labeled examples: each training instance is paired with the correct answer, and the model learns to predict that answer for new instances. This is the paradigm used in most classification and regression tasks, from image recognition to fraud detection to credit scoring. Unsupervised learning involves training a model on unlabeled data and letting it discover structure in the data on its own: identifying clusters of similar items, reducing data to its essential dimensions, or detecting anomalies. Reinforcement learning involves training a model through interaction with an environment, rewarding actions that lead to good outcomes and penalizing actions that lead to bad ones. This is the paradigm used to train AI systems that play games, control robots, and optimize complex systems.

Neural Networks and Deep Learning

A neural network is a computational architecture loosely inspired by the structure of biological brains. It consists of layers of mathematical units called neurons, each of which receives inputs, applies a mathematical transformation, and passes the result to the next layer. The network learns by adjusting the strengths (weights) of the connections between neurons, guided by a training signal that indicates whether the network's outputs are moving in the right direction.

Deep learning refers to the use of neural networks with many layers, “deep” in the sense of many sequential layers of processing. Deep neural networks are capable of learning complex, hierarchical representations of data: in image recognition, for example, early layers learn to detect simple features like edges and corners, middle layers learn to detect more complex features like shapes and textures, and later layers learn to detect high-level features like faces and objects. This hierarchical representation learning is what makes deep neural networks so effective at tasks that previously seemed impossibly complex for computers.

Large Language Models

A large language model (LLM) is a neural network trained on very large amounts of text data using a specific architecture called the Transformer, with a training objective centered on predicting the next token in a sequence. The "large" in LLM refers to both the size of the model (measured in the number of parameters, which range from hundreds of millions to hundreds of billions) and the size of the training dataset (which may comprise trillions of tokens of text from the internet, books, and other sources).

The remarkable capabilities of LLMs, their ability to answer questions, generate text, write code, and engage in reasoning across many domains, emerge from the combination of the Transformer architecture, which enables efficient learning of long-range dependencies in text, and the enormous scale of training, which exposes the model to enough text to develop rich internal representations of the world as described in human writing.

Narrow AI vs. General AI

Narrow AI (sometimes called weak AI or artificial narrow intelligence, ANI) refers to AI systems designed and trained to perform specific tasks within a defined domain. Every AI system that currently exists is narrow AI: a language model is trained for language tasks, an image recognition model is trained for visual tasks, a game-playing AI is trained for game-playing. However impressive within its domain, a narrow AI cannot generalize to tasks outside that domain without retraining.

Artificial general intelligence (AGI) refers to a hypothetical AI system that can perform any intellectual task that a human can perform, with no domain restriction and without specific training for each domain. AGI does not currently exist, and there is no consensus on when or whether it will exist. The term is sometimes used loosely to describe AI systems that are very capable across many domains; this usage conflates impressive narrow AI with the genuinely distinct concept of general intelligence.

Artificial superintelligence (ASI) refers to a hypothetical AI system that surpasses human intelligence across all domains. ASI is currently a theoretical concept discussed in AI safety research, not a description of any existing or near-term technology.

Key Practical Terms

Term	Definition
Parameters	The numerical values in a neural network that are adjusted during training. A model's size is often measured in parameters; more parameters generally mean greater capacity to learn complex patterns.
Token	The basic unit of text that a language model processes. Tokens are typically words or parts

	of words; roughly, one token corresponds to about 3/4 of a word in English.
Context window	The maximum amount of text that a model can process in a single pass. Models with larger context windows can handle longer documents and maintain coherence over longer conversations.
Fine-tuning	The process of continuing to train a pre-trained model on a smaller, task-specific dataset to specialize its capabilities for a particular use case.
Prompt	The input text provided to a language model, including any instructions, context, and examples that guide the model's response.
Inference	The process of using a trained model to generate outputs given new inputs, as distinct from the training process that produced the model.

RAG (Retrieval-Augmented Generation)	An architecture that combines a language model with a document retrieval system, allowing the model to retrieve relevant documents and use them to ground its responses in specific sources.
Embedding	A numerical representation of text (or other data) in a high-dimensional vector space, designed so that semantically similar content has similar numerical representations.
Temperature	A parameter that controls the randomness of a model's outputs. Lower temperature produces more deterministic, predictable outputs; higher temperature produces more varied, creative outputs.
Hallucination	The generation of fluent, confident-sounding output that is factually incorrect. A persistent feature of language models that requires management

	through verification practices.

Putting the Vocabulary to Work

Knowing a term's definition and knowing a term are different things. The gap closes only through active use. Three practices accelerate vocabulary internalization faster than passive reading. First, the substitution test: when you encounter the word “AI” in a headline or meeting, mentally substitute the more precise term. Is the headline actually about machine learning? A specific large language model? An agentic system? The substitution forces precision. Second, the explanation test: if you cannot explain a term to a non-technical colleague in under sixty seconds without jargon, you do not yet own it. Third, the challenge test: when a vendor, colleague, or news article uses a term imprecisely, note it. The ability to identify imprecision is a sign of genuine fluency.

If you hear...	The more precise term is often...
Artificial intelligence / AI	Machine learning, deep learning, large language model, or generative AI, depending on what is actually being described
AI thinks / understands / knows	The model predicts, generates, or pattern-matches, it does not think or understand in any human sense
AI hallucinated	The model generated a plausible-sounding but

	factually incorrect output, a structural feature of all current LLMs
We are using AI	We have deployed [specific tool or model] for [specific task], producing [specific output type]
AI will replace jobs	Specific categories of task within jobs are being automated; the role composition of many jobs is changing
Our AI is trained on your data	Your inputs may be used to fine-tune the model or improve training data, check the platform's data policy carefully

Develop the habit of asking one clarifying question whenever AI is discussed in a meeting or document: "Which specific tool or model are we referring to, and what is the task it is being used for?" This single question does more to improve organizational AI decision-making than any glossary.

✓ YOUR ACTION PLAN

DAYS 1-7: THIS WEEK

- Read the Glossary at the back of this book. Flag every term you cannot define in your own words without looking it up.
- Write a plain-English, one-sentence definition for each flagged term in your own words, not the glossary's. This is the beginning of your Personal AI Lexicon.
- Find one current AI news article and identify every technical term used. Confirm you can define each. Note any terms used imprecisely.
- Apply the substitution test from this chapter in your next meeting or email where AI is discussed.

DAYS 8-30: THIS MONTH

- Build your Personal AI Lexicon to at least 30 terms: new terms as you encounter them, each with a definition, an example, and a note on why it matters to your work.
- Complete the explanation test: explain the difference between machine learning, deep learning, and large language model to a non-technical colleague until they nod with genuine understanding.
- Start a Buzzword Watch List: imprecise AI terms you hear in your work context. For each, note the more accurate formulation you would use instead.

DAYS 31-90: THIS QUARTER

- Teach someone. Volunteer for a 10-minute AI vocabulary briefing at a team meeting or in a one-on-one. Teaching is the most powerful vocabulary retention tool that exists.
- Score yourself on the AI Manager Competency Self-Assessment in Chapter 17. This chapter builds the foundation for all other scores. Identify your gaps and plan your reading.

▸ GO DEEPER: sALLvit™ Certified AI Manager (CAM) Program

In the CAM program, AI vocabulary and conceptual literacy is applied through fill-in workbook exercises with peer vocabulary challenges and group definition tests that force active recall rather than passive reading. To practice this skill under facilitated conditions and earn the Certified AI Manager credential, visit **sallvit-corp.com** or email contact.us@sallvit-corp.com.

Key Takeaways: Chapter 11

- Machine learning encompasses supervised, unsupervised, and reinforcement learning, three distinct paradigms for teaching systems from data.

- Deep learning uses multi-layered neural networks to learn hierarchical representations of complex data.
- Large language models (LLMs) are transformer-based neural networks trained on massive text datasets; their remarkable capabilities emerge from scale and architecture together.
- Every current AI is narrow AI; AGI (artificial general intelligence) does not yet exist and its timeline is genuinely uncertain.
- Precision in AI vocabulary enables clearer thinking, better communication with technical teams, and more credible engagement with stakeholders.

CHAPTER 12

AI Is Everywhere

Recognizing the invisible technology that shapes your world

One of the most important perceptual shifts for an AI Manager is learning to see AI where it already exists. Most people think of AI as something new and separate, a chatbot you talk to, a system you explicitly use. But AI has been woven into the fabric of everyday life for more than a decade. The recommendation algorithm that decides what you see on social media, the navigation system that routes your commute, the fraud detection system that monitors your credit card, the speech recognition system on your phone, the filter that keeps spam out of your inbox: all of these are AI systems, most of them more sophisticated than the AI tools that get press coverage.

> *Any sufficiently advanced technology is indistinguishable from magic.*
>
> – *Arthur C. Clarke*

AI in Your Pocket

The smartphone in your pocket is the most sophisticated AI deployment most people interact with daily, and most people interact with it without thinking of it as AI at all. Voice assistants use AI for speech recognition and natural language understanding. The camera uses AI for scene recognition, face detection, portrait mode background separation, and image enhancement. The keyboard uses AI to predict your next word. The autocorrect system uses AI to identify and fix typos.

The battery management system uses AI to optimize charging based on your usage patterns. The spam filter in your messages uses AI. Even the way your photos are sorted and searchable uses AI face recognition and scene classification.

AI in Commerce

When you visit Amazon and see a list of "Customers who bought this also bought..." you are seeing collaborative filtering, one of the oldest and most commercially impactful machine learning applications. Netflix estimates that its recommendation engine saves more than $1 billion annually in customer retention by keeping subscribers engaged with relevant content. Spotify's Discover Weekly playlist, which generates a personalized 30-song playlist every Monday, uses machine learning to identify patterns in your listening history and match them to songs you have not heard. These recommendation systems are not merely convenient; they shape consumer behavior at enormous scale.[26]

Hiring and HR systems are increasingly AI-powered in ways that applicants rarely see and often do not know about. Applicant Tracking Systems (ATS) use AI to screen resumes, rank applicants, and filter out candidates who do not match keyword patterns. Video interview platforms use AI to analyze facial expressions, voice tone, and word choice during recorded interviews. These AI HR systems have been criticized for perpetuating bias in hiring and for making consequential decisions that candidates cannot meaningfully challenge. Understanding these systems is essential for both

---

[26]Gomez-Uribe, C. A., & Hunt, N. (2016). The Netflix Recommender System: Algorithms, Business Value, and Innovation. ACM Transactions on Management Information Systems, 6(4), 1-19. Netflix has reported the figure in various investor and research contexts.

job seekers and the AI Managers responsible for evaluating and overseeing them.

AI in Healthcare

Healthcare represents one of the most consequential and most promising domains for AI application. AI systems are now FDA-cleared for an expanding range of medical imaging applications: detecting diabetic retinopathy in eye scans, identifying pneumonia in chest X-rays, detecting breast cancer in mammograms, and analyzing echocardiograms for cardiac abnormalities. A 2020 study in Nature Medicine found that an AI system trained to detect breast cancer in mammograms outperformed a panel of six radiologists on a large UK dataset, while simultaneously reducing false positives.[27]

AI is also being used in drug discovery, where it can analyze molecular structures and predict drug-receptor interactions at a speed that dramatically accelerates the early stages of pharmaceutical development. DeepMind's AlphaFold, which solved the protein structure prediction problem in 2020, has already transformed structural biology research. Insilico Medicine used AI to identify a candidate drug for a fibrotic lung disease and bring it from initial discovery to Phase I clinical trials in under three years, a process that typically takes decades.[28]

---

[27]McKinney, S. M., Sieniek, M., Godbole, V., Godwin, J., Antropova, N., Ashrafian, H., et al. (2020). International evaluation of an AI system for breast cancer screening. Nature, 577, 89-94.

[28]Zhavoronkov, A., Ivanenkov, Y. A., Aliper, A., Veselov, M. S., Aladinskiy, V. A., Aladinskaya, A. V., et al. (2019). Deep learning enables rapid identification of potent DDR1 kinase inhibitors. Nature Biotechnology, 37, 1038-1040. Insilico Medicine subsequently advanced ISM001-055 to Phase II trials for IPF.

AI in Finance

Financial services were among the earliest industries to adopt machine learning at scale, driven by the combination of large structured datasets, high-stakes decisions, and quantifiable outcomes. Fraud detection systems at credit card companies use machine learning to identify unusual transaction patterns in real time, flagging potentially fraudulent transactions for human review before they are completed. These systems process millions of transactions per second and can identify subtle patterns of fraud that would be invisible to human analysts.

Algorithmic trading uses machine learning to identify and execute trading opportunities at speeds measured in microseconds. High-frequency trading firms use proprietary machine learning models to analyze market data, news feeds, and social media sentiment and execute trades that capture tiny price discrepancies across markets. AI is also used in credit scoring, insurance underwriting, regulatory compliance monitoring, and customer service, fundamentally changing the economics of financial services.

AI in Education

AI's role in education is expanding rapidly, and the implications for learning are profound and contested. Intelligent tutoring systems use AI to provide personalized instruction at each student's level, adjusting the difficulty and style of problems based on the student's performance. Carnegie Learning's MATHia platform, used by hundreds of thousands of students, uses AI to provide individualized math instruction and has been shown in rigorous studies to improve learning outcomes compared to traditional instruction.

On the other side of the equation, AI writing tools have created significant challenges for educational assessment. When students can produce essay-length text with the help of AI, traditional essay assignments become an unreliable measure of student learning. Educators are responding with a mix of strategies: redesigning assessments to focus on process rather than product, requiring in-class writing, using oral examinations, and developing AI literacy skills explicitly in curriculum. The AI Manager who works in educational contexts needs to be fluent in all of these debates.

The AI Opportunity Map: Auditing Your Professional Landscape

Before you can deploy AI strategically, you need an accurate picture of where AI already exists in your professional life and where the highest-value opportunities remain untapped. The AI Opportunity Map is a structured audit you conduct on your own role. It takes about an hour the first time, and should be repeated quarterly as the AI landscape evolves.

The audit has three components. The first is the Tool Inventory: list every software application you use in a typical work week and search each one for AI or automation features, whether active or dormant. Most professionals are using a fraction of the AI capability already inside their existing tools. The second component is the Task Analysis: for each of your major responsibilities, estimate the percentage of time spent on tasks that are routine and rule-based versus tasks that require genuine judgment, creativity, or relationship management. AI augmentation opportunity is highest where routine time is highest. The third component is the Industry Scan: identify five to ten AI applications currently being adopted by organizations in your field, and for each, assess whether your organization is ahead, at parity, or behind the curve.

AI Opportunity Map: Template	How to Complete It
TOOL INVENTORY: List every app you use weekly	Search each tool for AI features (look in Settings, Help, or release notes). Mark each: Active / Unused / Unknown
TASK ANALYSIS: List your top 5 responsibilities	For each, estimate: % routine/repeatable vs. % judgment-required. AI value is highest where routine % is high
CAPABILITY GAPS: Where do you lose time to repetitive work?	These are your highest-priority prompt engineering and automation targets from Chapters 14 and 16
INDUSTRY SCAN: Name 5 AI tools deployed in your field	For each: What problem does it solve? Who uses it? What are its known risks or limitations?
EXPOSURE RISK: Which of your tasks are most automatable?	These are not threats to avoid but skills to augment, knowing your exposure is the first step to managing it

The output of this audit is a one-page AI Opportunity Map document: your personal inventory of AI potential in your role and industry. This document becomes the foundation for every AI initiative you propose and every skill you prioritize developing. Update it every quarter. The map you draw today will look different in ninety days.

✓ YOUR ACTION PLAN

DAYS 1-7: THIS WEEK

- Conduct your AI Opportunity Map audit: list every software tool you use in a typical work week and search each for AI or automation features, active or dormant.
- Count how many AI-powered decisions touch your workflow in one day without your direct involvement (spam filter, content recommendations, fraud alerts, scheduling assists). The number is almost always higher than expected.
- Identify one AI feature inside a tool you already use that you have never turned on. Read its documentation before the week ends.

DAYS 8-30: THIS MONTH

- Activate and test the AI feature you identified this week. Document: what problem it solves, where it falls short, and whether it saves measurable time.
- Complete your Industry Scan: identify five AI tools currently being adopted in your field. For each, note the problem addressed,

the users, and the known limitations or risks.

- Write your completed AI Opportunity Map as a one-page document. Identify your two highest-value AI augmentation opportunities. These become your Ch. 14 and Ch. 15 priorities.

DAYS 31-90: THIS QUARTER

- Act on one high-value opportunity from your AI Opportunity Map. Implement an AI-assisted workflow for a task that currently consumes significant routine time. Document time saved.
- Share your AI Opportunity Map with a manager or trusted colleague. Propose one AI deployment in your team that would add clear, measurable value. This is your first formal AI initiative.
- Update your AI Opportunity Map. The landscape will have shifted. New tools will have launched. Treat this as a living document, not a one-time exercise.

▸ GO DEEPER: sALLvit™ Certified AI Manager (CAM) Program

In the CAM program, the AI Opportunity Map is applied through a live worksheet completed across all four professional tracks (Executive, Manager, Operator, and Specialist) with peer comparison and facilitated debrief on the highest-value opportunities identified. To practice this skill under facilitated conditions and earn the Certified AI Manager credential, visit **sallvit-corp.com** or email contact.us@sallvit-corp.com.

Key Takeaways: Chapter 12

- AI is already deeply embedded in everyday life, in smartphones, recommendation systems, hiring software, healthcare diagnostics, and financial systems.
- Recognizing existing AI deployments is essential for understanding the technology's actual capabilities and limitations.
- AI in healthcare is producing genuinely impressive results in medical imaging and drug discovery, but requires careful oversight and validation.
- AI in hiring raises serious fairness and accountability concerns that AI Managers in HR contexts need to address explicitly.
- The expansion of AI into education is creating both new opportunities for personalized learning and new challenges for assessment and academic integrity.

CHAPTER 13

Real or Fake? Navigating AI-Generated Content

Developing your detection instincts

The ability to distinguish AI-generated content from human-generated content is becoming one of the fundamental information literacy skills of the modern era. As AI generation quality improves and becomes more accessible, the cognitive effort required to detect AI-generated content increases, while the consequences of being deceived by it grow more significant. This chapter provides practical guidance on developing the detection instincts that every AI Manager needs.

> *A mind is like a parachute. It doesn't work if it is not open.*
>
> *– Frank Zappa*

Image Detection

AI image generation has improved dramatically, but current systems still produce characteristic artifacts that a trained eye can often detect. The most reliable tells in AI-generated images include: unnatural hands (fingers that are too long, fused, or the wrong number), inconsistent fine detail (particularly in hair, fur, text, and background elements), spatial incoherence in backgrounds and reflections, lighting inconsistencies where shadows and highlights do not match across the image, and a general quality of "over-smoothness" in skin and surfaces that real photography does not produce. Text within AI-generated images is a particularly reliable indicator: current image generators struggle to produce legible, correctly spelled text.

Technical tools for image authentication include reverse image search (to determine whether an image has appeared elsewhere and in what context), metadata inspection (AI-generated images often lack the EXIF metadata that cameras embed in photographs), and AI detection tools like Hive Moderation, Illuminarty, and AI or Not. These tools analyze statistical patterns in images that differ between AI-generated and camera-captured content. They are not infallible, but they can provide a useful second opinion when authenticity matters.

Video Detection

Deepfake video is technically more challenging to produce than still images, and typically more challenging to authenticate. Common tells include: inconsistent blinking (many early deepfakes had faces that blinked at unnatural intervals), visual artifacts at face boundaries where the synthesized face meets the original body, unnatural eye movements, lighting on the face that does not match the ambient lighting of the scene, and audio-visual synchronization issues where lip movements do not perfectly match the audio.

Advanced deepfakes may pass casual visual inspection, making technical authentication increasingly important. Tools like Microsoft's Video Authenticator and Intel's FakeCatcher analyze physiological signals (like the subtle color variations in skin that correspond to heartbeat) and statistical patterns in pixel values to detect synthetic video.

The FakeCatcher tool claims over 96 percent accuracy on the public deepfake benchmarks, though real-world performance on adversarially constructed deepfakes is typically lower.

Text Detection

Detecting AI-generated text is in some ways the hardest detection problem, because AI text generators can produce content that is indistinguishable from human writing in terms of content and style. The current generation of AI text detectors works by identifying statistical patterns in word choice, sentence structure, and perplexity (a measure of how predictable each word is given the words that precede it) that differ between AI-generated and human-generated text. Tools like GPTZero, Copyleaks, and Turnitin's AI detection feature use these approaches.

The fundamental limitation of AI text detection is that the technology that generates AI text and the technology that detects it are in an arms race, and the generators currently have the advantage. As generation models improve, detection becomes harder. A 2023 study by researchers at MIT found that AI text detectors had false positive rates of between three and six percent, meaning they flagged as AI-generated a significant proportion of text that was entirely human-written. For high-stakes decisions (like academic integrity judgments), relying solely on automated AI text detection without other evidence is problematic.[29]

Behavioral and contextual signals often provide more reliable indication of AI-generated text than technical detectors. AI-

---

[29]Liang, W., Yuksekgonul, M., Mao, Y., Wu, E., & Zou, J. (2023). GPT detectors are biased against non-native English writers. Patterns, 4(7), 100779. The MIT study referenced in this chapter found false positive rates of 3-6% for human-written academic text.

generated text tends to be unusually well-structured, unusually complete, unusually even in quality, and unusually free of the idiosyncratic errors and personality markers that characterize human writing. It tends to hedge in characteristic ways ("certainly," "of course," "absolutely" are overused by many AI systems). It tends to be comprehensive to a fault, covering all perspectives on a topic even when the prompt called for a specific stance. Developing sensitivity to these behavioral patterns is the most reliable long-term detection skill.

Building Your Content Verification Protocol

Detection skills are most valuable when they are institutionalized, not improvised. A Content Verification Protocol is a short, written checklist that defines the specific checks you or your team perform before publishing, distributing, or acting on any externally-sourced content. Developing this protocol forces you to think systematically about where synthetic content poses risk in your specific context, and it creates a repeatable standard that others can follow.

The protocol should be calibrated to stakes. A low-stakes internal email needs different verification than a press release or a legal filing. For each content type in your work, define the minimum acceptable verification standard. The following framework provides a starting point that you should adapt to your context.

Verification Level	When to Apply It and What to Check
LEVEL 1: QUICK SCAN (2 minutes)	Check author/source credibility. Run a

Low-stakes internal use	reverse image search if images are included. Look for AI text tells: unusual completeness, hedging phrases, uniform quality throughout.
LEVEL 2: STANDARD REVIEW (15 minutes) External-facing, moderate stakes	All Level 1 checks, plus: verify at least three specific factual claims against authoritative sources. Check image metadata. Run text through one AI detection tool and note the verdict.
LEVEL 3: FULL AUDIT (60+ minutes) High-stakes: legal, financial, medical, regulatory	All Level 2 checks, plus: subject-matter expert review of all claims. Full citation verification. Image forensic analysis if images are evidentiary. Document your verification process for the record.
RED FLAGS requiring immediate escalation	No identifiable author or source. Images with text artifacts or spatial incoherence. Claims that are unverifiable or contradict established sources. Content that arrived unsolicited and is unusually persuasive.

Publish your Content Verification Protocol to your team as a one-page document. The act of writing it makes your implicit verification instincts explicit and teachable. The act of sharing it starts a conversation about AI content risk that most organizations have not yet had.

✓ YOUR ACTION PLAN

DAYS 1-7: THIS WEEK

- Run the hands test: examine ten AI-generated images and ten real photographs. Before using any detection tool, identify your own verdict on each. Then check your results against a free detection tool (Hive Moderation or AI or Not). Score your accuracy and note where you were fooled.
- Read one article from an unfamiliar source and deliberately look for AI text tells: unusual completeness, consistent quality throughout, characteristic hedging phrases. Log what you notice.
- Begin your Detection Tells Log: a running document where you record AI-generation artifacts you encounter in text, images, and video. Aim for at least three entries per week.

DAYS 8-30: THIS MONTH

- Draft your Content Verification Protocol using the three-level framework from this chapter. Calibrate each level to the actual content types and stakes in your specific work context.

- Test an AI text detector (GPTZero or Copyleaks) on samples you know to be human-written and AI-generated. Evaluate its accuracy and false-positive rate. Note its limitations.
- Share your Content Verification Protocol with at least one colleague. Discuss one situation in your work where it should have been applied but was not.

DAYS 31-90: THIS QUARTER

- Formalize your Content Verification Protocol as a one-page team document. Present it to your team or manager as a governance proposal. This is your first AI policy artifact.
- Identify and flag one instance of AI-generated content in your professional environment that was presented or treated as human-generated. Document it without accusation. The observation itself is valuable.

AI Content Red Flags: A Practical Checklist

- VOCABULARY MARKERS: Words like "delve," "tapestry," "landscape," "crucial," "beacon," "dynamic," and "testament" appear at statistically elevated rates in AI-generated text. Their presence alone is not proof of AI authorship, but a document containing several of them warrants scrutiny.

- EVEN QUALITY THROUGHOUT: Human writing has rhythm, variation, and the occasional rough sentence. AI-generated text tends toward uniform quality throughout, no weak paragraphs, no sudden brilliance, no stylistic irregularity. Suspiciously consistent quality is itself a signal.
- NO SPECIFIC ANECDOTES OR NAMED EXAMPLES: AI defaults to generic examples and hypothetical scenarios. Human experts reach for specific named cases, dates, colleagues, and incidents. A professional document that contains no specific, verifiable anecdotes is a candidate for scrutiny.
- CHARACTERISTIC HEDGING PATTERNS: AI models hedge in predictable ways: "it is worth noting that," "it is important to consider," "of course," "while this is not universally true." These phrases appear because RLHF training penalizes overconfident outputs. A document saturated with this hedging pattern may be AI-generated.
- UNUSUAL COMPLETENESS: AI responds to every subpart of a request with the same

depth and competence. Human subject matter experts are deep in some areas and shallow in others. A response that is equally fluent across a dozen distinct subtopics is statistically unusual for a human author.

- IMAGES: Check for spatial incoherence (hands with extra fingers, text that is unreadable, backgrounds that contradict themselves), lighting that does not match the scene, and edge artifacts around hair and complex boundaries. Run a reverse image search before trusting any image from an unfamiliar source.

▸ GO DEEPER: sALLvit™ Certified AI Manager (CAM) Program

In the CAM program, AI content detection and verification is applied through a live red-team exercise using real synthetic samples, including an echo chamber demonstration with primary source override, so participants can experience the failure mode firsthand rather than reading about it. To practice this skill under facilitated conditions and earn the Certified AI Manager credential, visit **sallvit-corp.com** or email contact.us@sallvit-corp.com.

Key Takeaways: Chapter 13

- AI image artifacts (hands, text, over-smooth textures) provide reliable detection cues that improve with practice.
- Deepfake video detection relies on both visual tells and technical tools analyzing physiological signals and pixel statistics.
- AI text detection tools are useful but imperfect; false positive rates of 3-6% make them unreliable for high-stakes judgments without supporting evidence.
- Behavioral patterns, unusual completeness, characteristic hedging, even quality throughout, often provide more reliable AI text detection than automated tools.
- Detection skills are a moving target as generation technology improves; the most durable skill is critical evaluation of content provenance and context.

CHAPTER 14

Mastering the Art of Prompt Engineering

The skill that defines the AI Manager

If there is a single skill that defines the practical value of an AI Manager, it is prompt engineering: the ability to craft precise, effective instructions that reliably guide AI systems toward the outputs you want. Prompt engineering is simultaneously more important and more subtle than most people expect. A bad prompt can make a very capable AI produce useless output. A great prompt can make a modestly capable AI produce extraordinary output. The difference between the two is the prompt engineer's skill, and it is a skill that can be learned, practiced, and refined.

The term "prompt engineering" is slightly misleading in that it suggests an exclusively technical process. In reality, it is as much a communication skill as a technical one: the art of expressing precisely what you want, anticipating how the AI will interpret your words, providing the context needed to eliminate ambiguity, and structuring the request in a way that channels the AI's capabilities toward your goal. Great prompt engineers are, at their core, great communicators who understand the specific communication patterns that AI systems respond to most effectively.

▶ **TRY THIS NOW**

Pause here. This experiment takes about two minutes.

Step 1: The Search Query

Open a web browser and search this exact phrase: "AI writing tools for beginners" Spend fifteen seconds scanning the first page of results. Notice what you see: sponsored listings, article headlines like "The 10 Best AI Writers in 2025," product comparison sites, ads. You now have a map of the landscape. You still have to navigate it yourself.

Step 2: The AI Prompt

Now open any AI chatbot (ChatGPT, Claude, Gemini, or any other) and type this exactly: "I write a weekly internal newsletter for a 200-person company. I have no technical background. Which single AI writing tool would save me the most time on first drafts, and what is the one mistake most beginners make when using it? Give me a direct recommendation, not a list." Read the response.

Step 3: Compare the Two

You got different things. The search returned pointers to content written by other humans, ranked by relevance signals and commercial interest, that you must read and evaluate yourself. The AI prompt returned a direct, reasoned answer calibrated to your specific situation, role, and constraint, in seconds. Same underlying question. Completely different output.

> ✍ **What you just experienced:** Search queries retrieve. Prompts converse. A search is a question you ask the internet; a prompt is a task you assign a collaborator. The search engine indexes the world's existing answers. The AI constructs a new answer for you. Neither is universally better; for finding a specific webpage or verifying a fact, search wins. For getting a direct, context-aware response to an ambiguous problem, the prompt wins. The rest of this chapter is about making those prompts as powerful as possible.

> *If you can only ask one question, it should always be Why?!*
>
> – *Anonymous*

Principle 1: Clarity

Clarity means using precise language that leaves no ambiguity about what you are asking for. The most common source of poor AI output is a vague prompt that could be interpreted in multiple ways, leading the AI to pick one interpretation (often not the one you intended) and produce output accordingly. Reviewing your prompts before submitting them with the question "Could this be interpreted differently from how I intend it?" and refining any ambiguities you find will dramatically improve your output quality.

Clarity also means being explicit about constraints and exclusions. If you do not want the AI to use jargon, say so. If you do not want the AI to discuss a certain aspect of the topic, say so. If you want the AI to take a specific perspective, say so. AI systems will not infer unstated preferences; they will produce the most statistically probable response to what you actually wrote, which may be very different from what you meant.

Instead of...	Use...
Tell me about this battle.	Summarize the Battle of Gettysburg in three bullet points, focusing on the strategic decisions made by each commanding general.
Write something about climate change.	Write a 300-word informational paragraph about the economic costs of climate change for a general adult audience, citing at least two specific examples.
Make this better.	Revise the following paragraph to be more concise (under 50 words), use active voice throughout, and eliminate all jargon.

Principle 2: Specificity

Specificity means defining the scope, constraints, and parameters of your request in enough detail that the AI can produce exactly what you need rather than something in the general neighborhood of what you need. Specificity includes:

the length or word count of the output, the format (paragraph, list, table, code), the audience (expert, general, child), the tone (formal, casual, persuasive, neutral), the perspective (first person, third person, specific role), and any technical constraints (specific frameworks, languages, or standards).

The counterintuitive lesson of specificity is that more specific prompts almost always produce better outputs, even though writing a detailed prompt takes more time. A two-sentence prompt that takes two minutes to write typically produces output that requires significant editing. A detailed prompt that takes five minutes to write typically produces output that requires little or no editing. The investment in specificity pays back immediately in time saved on output refinement.

Principle 3: Context

Context means providing the background information that the AI needs to understand your request in the way you intend. Context includes who you are and your relationship to the task ("As a nurse writing patient education materials..."), what the output will be used for ("...for patients recently diagnosed with Type 2 diabetes..."), any relevant prior work or information ("...following the guidelines in the attached protocol..."), and any constraints imposed by the context ("...at a sixth-grade reading level...").

System prompts, available in many AI platforms, are a particularly powerful form of context. A system prompt is text that is inserted before your actual query and provides standing instructions and context that apply to the entire conversation. A well-crafted system prompt can transform a general-purpose AI into a domain-specific expert, a specific communication style, or a role with specific responsibilities and constraints. If you use AI tools regularly for similar tasks, developing effective system prompts for those tasks is one of the highest-return investments you can make.

Principle 4: Goal Orientation

Goal orientation means being explicit about the outcome you want from the interaction, not just the task you are assigning. "Explain quantum entanglement" is a task description. "Explain quantum entanglement in a way that would allow my fifteen-year-old nephew to explain it to a friend the next day" is a goal-oriented request that constrains the output in a much more useful way. The goal specifies not just what content to produce but what level of understanding it should produce in a reader with specific characteristics.

Asking the AI to specify its own success criteria can be a powerful extension of goal orientation. Try: "Before you write this business proposal, tell me what criteria you think a successful proposal for this situation should meet." The AI will often articulate criteria that help you evaluate the output more precisely, and if its criteria are wrong, correcting them before the output is written is far more efficient than correcting the output after it is written.

Principle 5: Open-Endedness When Appropriate

While specificity and goal orientation are usually virtues in prompting, there are situations where a more open-ended prompt produces better results. Creative exploration, brainstorming, and initial ideation often benefit from prompts that give the AI latitude to explore rather than constraining it toward a specific output. "Generate ten different approaches to this marketing problem, ranging from conservative to unconventional" is a more useful brainstorming prompt than one that specifies exactly what kind of approaches you want, because the point is to discover options you had not already thought of.

Open-endedness is also valuable when you are uncertain about what you want. Asking the AI to "present three different ways I could structure this presentation, with the pros and cons of each" when you are not sure which structure is best leverages the AI's ability to rapidly generate alternatives while preserving your own judgment about which is best.

Principle 6: Format Requests

AI systems will produce whatever format is statistically most common in their training data for prompts like yours, which may not be the format you need. Explicitly specifying the format, "Provide this as a bulleted list of no more than ten items", "Structure this as a table with columns for X, Y, and Z", "Write this as a numbered step-by-step guide", ensures that the output is immediately usable rather than requiring reformatting.

For technical outputs, format requests can be even more specific: "Write this as a Python function with a docstring explaining its inputs and outputs," or "Return the answer as a JSON object with the following structure: { 'summary': string, 'key_points': array of strings, 'confidence': number from 0 to 1 }." This kind of structured output specification makes AI outputs directly machine-readable and usable in automated workflows.

The RTCFCS Prompt Framework

The six principles outlined in this chapter become most useful when they are combined into a single, repeatable structure you apply before writing any significant prompt. In the sALLvit™ AI Manager Certification Program, this structure is branded as RTCFCS: Role, Task, Context, Format, Constraints, and Success Criteria. The book presents these elements in a slightly different pedagogical sequence, but the components are identical. Knowing the RTCFCS name creates a direct bridge to the course's live prompting exercises and practical lab. The Prompt Template Framework below is not a formula to follow mechanically. It is a checklist to consult: for any given prompt, some elements will matter more than others. A simple factual query needs only clarity and specificity. A complex analysis or document generation task benefits from all six. With practice, moving through the framework takes thirty seconds and consistently produces better output than writing without it.

Framework Element	Fill In Before You Prompt
ROLE: Who should the AI be?	**Example: "You are an experienced employment lawyer specializing in US federal labor law."** Skip if: your query is purely factual and role context would add no value.
CONTEXT: What does the AI need to know about your situation?	**Example: "I am preparing for a mediation hearing on Thursday. The dispute involves a non-compete clause signed in 2019."**

	Skip if: the task is self-contained and context-independent.
TASK: What specific action do you want?	**Example: "Identify the three strongest arguments the other party is likely to make, and draft a one-paragraph rebuttal for each."** Never skip: this is the core of every prompt.
FORMAT: How should the output look?	**Example: "Present as a numbered list. Each item: argument summary (one sentence) followed by rebuttal (two to three sentences)."** Skip if: any format is equally useful.
CONSTRAINTS: What should the AI exclude or avoid?	**Example: "Do not cite cases older than 2015. Do not give legal advice; frame everything as analysis."** Skip if: you have no meaningful exclusions.
SUCCESS CRITERIA: What does a good response look like?	**Example: "A strong response will be specific enough that I could rehearse the rebuttals verbatim,**

not general observations."

Use when: you are unsure if the AI will interpret the task at the right level of depth.

Once you have filled in the elements that matter for your task, assemble them in order: Role, Context, Task, Format, Constraints, Success Criteria. Read the assembled prompt aloud before submitting it. If it sounds vague when spoken, it will produce a vague output. Revise until it sounds like a clear brief to a capable colleague. That is the standard.

Advanced Techniques: Chain-of-Thought

Chain-of-thought prompting instructs the AI to reason step-by-step before producing a final answer. This technique dramatically improves performance on reasoning tasks, mathematical problems, and complex analysis. The basic version is as simple as adding "Let's think step by step" to your prompt, which encourages the model to make its reasoning process explicit rather than jumping directly to a conclusion.[30]

More sophisticated versions of chain-of-thought prompting provide an explicit reasoning scaffold: "Analyze this problem using the following steps: first, identify the key stakeholders and their interests; second, identify the constraints imposed by each stakeholder; third, identify potential solutions that

---

[30]Wei, J., Wang, X., Schuurmans, D., Bosma, M., Xia, F., Chi, E., et al. (2022). Chain-of-Thought Prompting Elicits Reasoning in Large Language Models. Advances in Neural Information Processing Systems, 35. The paper showed consistent gains on arithmetic, symbolic, and commonsense reasoning benchmarks.

satisfy the most important constraints; fourth, evaluate each solution against all constraints and recommend the best one." This kind of structured reasoning prompt produces higher-quality analysis than an unstructured prompt for the same question.

Advanced Techniques: Few-Shot Prompting

Few-shot prompting means providing the AI with examples of the kind of output you want before asking it to produce a new instance. If you want the AI to write product descriptions in a specific style, providing two or three examples of product descriptions in that style dramatically improves the model's ability to match it. This is more efficient than trying to describe the style in abstract terms, because the model can learn more from examples than from descriptions.[31]

Few-shot prompting is particularly valuable when you are working with specialized formats, styles, or conventions that may not be well-represented in the model's training data. Providing examples ensures that the model understands what you actually want, rather than defaulting to the nearest common format in its training distribution.

Platform-Specific Tips

Different AI platforms have specific features that reward platform-specific prompting approaches. Google's Gemini, for instance, supports the use of the "@" symbol to direct the model to use specific integrated apps: "@Gmail find me all emails about the Project Aurora launch in the past 60 days." This makes Gemini particularly powerful in workflows that

---

[31]Brown, T., Mann, B., Ryder, N., Subbiah, M., Kaplan, J. D., Dhariwal, P., et al. (2020). Language Models are Few-Shot Learners. Advances in Neural Information Processing Systems, 33.

span multiple Google Workspace applications, as it can seamlessly combine data from Gmail, Drive, Calendar, and other services in a single response.

Many platforms support the use of code blocks in prompts to specify exact formatting requirements or to provide structured data. Providing data in a clearly formatted code block reduces the model's tendency to misinterpret or reformat the data. When asking for code output, specifying the language and version explicitly ("Write this in Python 3.11 using the requests library") produces more reliable output than leaving the language choice to the model.

Essential Habits: Four Tips Every AI User Should Build

Beyond frameworks and techniques, the highest-performing AI users share a small number of practical habits that protect their work and their time. These are not advanced strategies; they are operational hygiene. Build them early and they become automatic.

Tip 1: Save Your Prompts for Key Workflows

- Every time you write a prompt that produces genuinely good output for a recurring task, save it. Copy it to a dedicated document, a personal prompt library, or even a simple notes file. Label it with the task type, the platform it was written for, and the date.
- Most professionals write the same prompts dozens of times from scratch across their

careers, each time reinventing something they already solved. A saved prompt library is compounding intellectual capital: every entry saves future time and provides a tested starting point rather than a blank page.

- Organize your library by task type (writing, analysis, research, communication, code). For each entry note the platform, the framework used (Prompt Template or DVSA), and any known limitations or failure modes. Review and prune the library quarterly as platforms evolve.

Tip 2: Save Locally. Servers Fail.

- AI platforms are web-based services. Server outages, internet interruptions, browser crashes, and session timeouts happen. When they happen mid-session, unsaved work is gone. Every significant AI-assisted work product should be copied to a local file before the session ends.
- The discipline is simple: whenever you have generated something worth keeping, select all, copy, and paste it into a local document before doing anything else. Do not wait until the end of a long session. Save incrementally, exactly as you would with any important document.

- This habit also protects against platform-specific risks: accounts locked for payment issues, platform shutdowns, or policy changes that alter access. Your local copy belongs to you regardless of what happens to the platform.

Tip 3: One Task at a Time

- AI models can appear to handle multiple simultaneous requests, but quality degrades when a single prompt asks the AI to do too many distinct things at once. When given five instructions simultaneously, the model prioritizes some, abbreviates others, and occasionally conflates elements from different parts of the request.
- The professional standard is to break complex work into sequential single-task prompts. Complete the first task, review the output, then prompt for the next task. This approach produces better output at each step, makes errors easier to isolate and correct, and aligns with the DVSA Steer principle of targeted revision rather than global rewriting.
- A useful rule of thumb: if your prompt contains more than two ANDs, split it. Each AND represents a new task that deserves its

> own prompt, its own output, and its own quality review.

A Complete Workflow: The DVSA Framework

The Prompt Template Framework covered earlier in this chapter is about construction: how to build a prompt that gives the AI clear instructions. The DVSA Framework addresses a different and equally important question: what do you do after the prompt? DVSA stands for Draft, Verify, Steer, and Adjust. It is a four-stage workflow that covers the full lifecycle of a high-quality AI collaboration, from the first prompt to the final published output. Where the Prompt Template Framework is about engineering the input, DVSA is about managing the entire process. Together, they represent a complete professional methodology.

The framework's core insight is that interacting with AI effectively requires a shift in mental posture: from passive chatting to active engineering and auditing. The AI is not a conversational partner who gradually comes to understand you. It is, as the framework puts it, a highly competent specialized contractor who lacks institutional memory and requires exhaustive onboarding instructions for every session. DVSA operationalizes that posture across four sequential stages.

DVSA Stage	Objective and Core Mindset
STAGE 1: DRAFT Create a good prompt	Construct a deterministic boundary around the AI's

probabilistic engine to maximize the quality of the initial raw material. Do not ask questions; assign a mandate. Use professional role anchors, structural markup to isolate instructions from source data, explicit negative rules (tell the AI what not to do), and a specified output schema. The goal is not a good conversation opener but a complete brief that leaves no room for the AI to guess your intent.

STAGE 2: VERIFY
Validate the results

Perform a rigorous quality assurance audit on the draft, adopting a Zero-Trust posture: assume errors exist until you have verified they do not. The operator is 100% responsible for output accuracy. Conduct a grounding audit (cross-reference every statistic and claim against source documents), test structural format integrity (check JSON brackets, table columns, schema adherence), and apply factual stress-

	testing (question whether the AI's logical transitions relied on information that was not present in the input).
STAGE 3: STEER Iterate and redirect	Guide the model through incremental course corrections without restarting from scratch. Prompting is a collaborative conversation; treat the AI as a team member who needs specific, constructive feedback on a particular section, not a global rewrite. Execute sectional revisions targeting exact paragraphs. Inject corrective datasets mid-session when the model drifts. Use adversarial counter-prompting: ask the model to argue against its own recommendation and identify two potential failure modes of the plan it just produced.
STAGE 4: ADJUST Polish the final product	Transform the raw AI draft into a human-quality final artifact. AI output is raw material; the human contribution is what adds unique

perspective, authentic voice, and strategic value. Remove AI vocabulary signatures (words like “delve,” “tapestry,” “crucial,” “landscape,” “beacon,” and “excited” signal automated generation to any experienced reader). Inject proprietary insights, first-hand experience, and organizational context that no AI could supply. Align the output format to its final destination: slide deck, executive email, technical document, or CRM record.

Stage 1 in Detail: Drafting With Structural Precision

The DVSA Draft stage extends the principles of the RTCFCS Prompt Framework with one additional technique that has significant practical impact: structural markup. By wrapping different types of input in clearly labeled delimiters, you prevent the model from blending your instructions with your source data, a failure mode that produces confused, inconsistent output. A prompt that says “Summarize this financial report” followed by the raw report text will often produce an output that mixes the model's interpretation of the summary task with its interpretation of what a financial report summary should look like generically. A prompt that wraps the report in XML tags, providing an instruction block and a separate data block, gives the model clear boundaries: the instruction is in one container, the data it should summarize is in another, and the two cannot blur together.

Negative rules deserve special attention in the Draft stage. AI models have a structural tendency to fill gaps with plausible-sounding content, which means that any area of your prompt that is silent on a constraint will be filled with the model's best guess about what you want. The best-guess default is rarely wrong in a dramatic way; it is wrong in a subtle way that looks right until you scrutinize it. Explicit negative rules close those gaps before the model reaches them. Phrases like "Do not use industry buzzwords or speculative future forecasts" or "If data is absent, write [DATA ABSENT] rather than inferring" are not defensive boilerplate. They are precision engineering.

Stage 3 in Detail: Steering Without Restarting

The Steer stage addresses one of the most common and most costly mistakes in AI collaboration: the global rewrite. When an output is partially correct, the instinct is to discard it and start over with a better prompt. This instinct is expensive. A global rewrite discards the parts of the output that were correct and introduces new random variation across the entire response. Sectional revision is almost always the better approach: identify the specific section that needs correction, provide explicit feedback on what is wrong and what is needed, and ask the model to revise that section only, leaving the rest intact.

Adversarial counter-prompting is the Steer stage's most powerful technique and the least commonly used. After receiving a recommendation, analysis, or plan, ask the model: "Provide the strongest possible counter-argument to what you just recommended, and identify two specific failure modes of this approach." This technique does several things simultaneously. It tests whether the model's original position was robust or merely plausible. It surfaces objections you might not have thought to raise. And it models the kind of critical engagement that distinguishes strategic AI use from passive consumption. An AI manager who never asks the AI to argue against itself is using only half the tool.

Stage 4 in Detail: The Human Finishing Layer

The Adjust stage is where the AI collaboration becomes yours. Every AI-generated draft carries the statistical fingerprints of its training data: vocabulary choices that cluster around common patterns, structural tendencies toward particular opening and closing formulations, and a characteristic absence of the specific, the anecdotal, and the proprietary. The AI cannot tell your story. It does not know about the deployment that failed because team adoption lagged when training was delivered remotely rather than in person. It does not know about the client relationship that took eighteen months to repair after a miscalculation in a deliverable. It does not know what your organization has learned at cost. Injecting those proprietary insights into the AI's structural skeleton is what produces output that is genuinely valuable rather than generically competent.

The AI vocabulary sweep is worth doing systematically rather than impressionistically. Maintain a personal list of words and phrases that signal AI authorship to you when you encounter them in published content, and search for those words before finalizing any AI-assisted document. The list in the original DVSA framework (delve, testament, lighthouse, beacon, landscape, tapestry, excited, crucial, dynamic) is a starting point, not a complete inventory. Add to it as you develop your own detection instincts. The goal is not to disguise the fact that AI was involved in producing the work; it is to ensure that the final output reflects your judgment and your voice, which is the contribution that no model can replicate.

The two frameworks in this chapter are not rivals. They are complements that operate at different levels. The Prompt Template Framework is the foundation: it structures the individual prompt, from the role you assign the AI through to your success criteria. DVSA is the workflow: it manages the full collaboration session from first draft to final published output. A sophisticated AI Manager uses both, selecting the depth of rigor appropriate to the task. For a quick draft email, a well-constructed prompt is sufficient. For a multi-session research synthesis, client deliverable, or policy document, layering the DVSA workflow on top provides the end-to-end discipline that keeps the work grounded and human-quality throughout.

✓ YOUR ACTION PLAN

DAYS 1-7: THIS WEEK

- Complete the Search vs. Prompt exercise in this chapter if you have not done so already.
- Identify your three most time-consuming recurring tasks that involve writing, analysis, or research. For each, write a detailed prompt using the six-element Prompt Template Framework: Role, Context, Task, Format, Constraints, Success Criteria.
- Run each task twice: once with a vague one-sentence prompt, once with your structured

prompt. Save both outputs. The difference is your first prompt engineering evidence.

DAYS 8-30: THIS MONTH

- Build your Personal Prompt Library to 20 entries organized by task type (writing, analysis, research, code, communication) and rate each 1-5 for output consistency.
- Write system prompts for your top three recurring task types. Test each across three different sessions to evaluate reliability.
- Practice chain-of-thought prompting on one complex analysis task. Compare the output to a direct-answer prompt on the same question. Document what changed.
- Apply the DVSA Steer stage to one AI output this month: instead of discarding a partially correct draft, identify the specific section that needs revision, provide explicit feedback, and request a targeted rewrite of that section only. Note the difference in quality and efficiency versus starting over.

DAYS 31-90: THIS QUARTER

- Develop a one-page Prompt Standards Guide for your team: five to eight templates for your most common shared tasks, noting whether the task calls for a carefully structured prompt, the full DVSA workflow, or a combination of both, with usage notes and known failure modes.

- Share and teach your prompting approach to at least one colleague. Invite them to share prompts back. A shared prompt library compounds in value with every contributor.
- Contribute your best prompt to a professional community or publish it with commentary on why it works and which framework it uses. Teaching others solidifies your own expertise.

▸ GO DEEPER: sALLvit™ Certified AI Manager (CAM) Program

In the CAM program, the RTCFCS Prompt Framework and DVSA workflow is applied through the 7-phase Corporate Offsite Practical Lab, a 105-minute exercise involving real arithmetic verification, multi-model red teaming, contrast prompting demonstrations, and production of a final executive-ready deliverable. To practice this skill under facilitated conditions and earn the Certified AI Manager credential, visit **sallvit-corp.com** or email contact.us@sallvit-corp.com.

Key Takeaways: Chapter 14

- Prompt engineering is the most important practical skill for an AI Manager, a blend of communication skill and AI-specific technique.

- The six core principles: Clarity, Specificity, Context, Goal Orientation, Format Requests, and Assuming No Prior Knowledge.
- Chain-of-thought prompting (reasoning step-by-step) dramatically improves performance on complex reasoning tasks.
- Few-shot prompting (providing examples) is more effective than describing abstract style requirements.
- Platform-specific features like Gemini's @ syntax, system prompts, and structured output specification enable powerful workflow automation.
- The RTCFCS Prompt Framework (Role, Task, Context, Format, Constraints, Success Criteria) is the best default for most professional prompting tasks.
- The DVSA Framework (Draft, Verify, Steer, Adjust) manages the full collaboration lifecycle, from first prompt to final published output. It shifts the operator from passive chatting to active engineering and auditing.
- DVSA Stage 2 (Verify) requires a Zero-Trust posture: the operator is 100% responsible for output accuracy. Stage 3 (Steer) uses sectional revision and adversarial counter-prompting rather than global rewrites.

Stage 4 (Adjust) injects proprietary voice, removes AI vocabulary signatures, and adds organizational context no model can supply.

- The two frameworks complement each other: the RTCFCS Prompt Framework structures the individual prompt; DVSA governs the complete collaboration session from first draft to final output. A sophisticated AI Manager uses both.

CHAPTER 15

Choosing Your AI Stack

The right tool for the right task

The AI tool landscape in 2025 is more varied, more capable, and more confusing than ever before. Dozens of AI platforms compete for attention, each with genuine strengths, genuine weaknesses, and marketing that emphasizes the former while minimizing the latter. Choosing the right AI tools for your specific needs, and developing the judgment to use them appropriately rather than reflexively, which is one of the core competencies of an AI Manager. This chapter provides a practical guide to the major platforms and the principles for selecting among them.

> *The best solutions include we, not just me.*
>
> – *Anonymous*

The Major Platforms

OpenAI's ChatGPT/GPT-4 family remains one of the most capable and widely deployed AI platforms. GPT-4 demonstrates strong performance across virtually all language tasks, writing, analysis, coding, reasoning, and conversation, and its integration with the web through browsing, with code execution through the Advanced Data Analysis feature, and with external tools through the plugin ecosystem makes it among the most versatile options available. Its limitations include occasional hallucination (as with all LLMs), a knowledge cutoff that may leave it unaware of recent events (mitigated by web browsing), and higher cost compared to some alternatives.

Google's Gemini platform leverages Google's unique advantages: deep integration with the Google Workspace ecosystem (Gmail, Drive, Docs, Sheets, Calendar), access to real-time search results, and a multimodal architecture that handles text, images, audio, and video natively. Gemini Ultra (the most capable model tier) demonstrates particularly strong performance on reasoning benchmarks. For users who work primarily in the Google ecosystem, Gemini's integrations provide workflow efficiency that is difficult to replicate with other tools.

Anthropic's Claude has earned a strong reputation for safety, nuanced reasoning, and the handling of long and complex documents. Claude's context window (100,000+ tokens in Claude 3) allows it to process documents far longer than most competing models can handle, a significant advantage for legal document review, long-form research synthesis, and complex multi-document analysis. Claude tends to be more cautious than some alternatives in declining to assist with potentially harmful requests, which is an advantage in organizational deployments but can occasionally be frustrating for legitimate edge cases.

Microsoft's Copilot, powered by GPT-4, is deeply integrated into the Microsoft 365 ecosystem. For organizations already operating in Microsoft's environment, using Teams, Outlook, Word, Excel, and PowerPoint, Copilot provides AI assistance directly within the tools employees are already using, reducing the friction of AI adoption. The ability to reference specific documents, emails, and meeting transcripts in Copilot queries makes it particularly valuable for enterprise knowledge management.

The Pander Problem: AI and Engagement

Every major AI platform is designed, to some degree, to maximize user engagement. This creates a systematic tendency toward a behavior that might be called "pandering": the AI adapts its responses to what the user appears to want to hear, validating the user's views, agreeing with the user's assessments, and softening disagreements to a point where they cease to be useful. This is not a deliberate design choice in most cases; it is an emergent consequence of training processes that reward responses that users rate positively, and users tend to rate validating responses more positively than challenging ones.

The AI Manager needs to actively counteract the pander dynamic in their AI usage. Specific techniques include explicitly requesting devil's advocate analysis ("Assume my approach is wrong. What are the strongest arguments against it?"), requiring the AI to provide evidence for its assessments rather than just assertions ("List three pieces of evidence that would cause you to change this recommendation"), and alternating between AI tools with different training distributions to compare their responses on contested questions. Developing a habit of asking the AI to challenge your assumptions rather than confirm them is one of the most valuable skills an AI Manager can cultivate.

The Three-Layer Bias Architecture

Platform differences in AI output go deeper than dataset choices. Every major AI platform produces different outputs for the same prompt, and not just because of what it was trained on. There are three distinct layers where bias is introduced, and understanding all three changes how you interpret and cross-check AI output.

Bias Layer	What It Is and What It Produces
LAYER 1: DATASET BIAS What texts went in	The foundational layer. The model reflects the biases, gaps, perspectives, and factual errors in its training data. If the training data over-represents certain demographics, cultures, geographies, or time periods, the model's default outputs will reflect that imbalance. Dataset bias is largely invisible to the user but shapes every default response.
LAYER 2: RLHF BIAS Who rated the outputs	Reinforcement Learning from Human Feedback introduces a second bias layer: the perspectives, preferences, and blind spots of the human reviewers who rated model outputs during training. The demographics, cultural context, and professional background of those reviewers directly shaped which outputs were rated positively and which were

	penalized. A model trained with RLHF reviewers from a narrow demographic will reflect the preferences of that group even on topics where it has broad training data.
LAYER 3: ALGORITHMIC WEIGHTING BIAS What the platform tuned	The final layer is deliberate: every AI platform makes explicit choices about what to amplify and what to suppress through fine-tuning, safety filters, and content policies. These choices are proprietary and vary significantly between platforms. Claude emphasizes caution and epistemic humility. Grok emphasizes directness and lower content filtering. These are not natural differences; they are designed ones. Knowing this, you can route tasks to the platform whose tuning most closely matches what you need.

The practical takeaway is a simple rule: for any consequential output, treat platform differences as diagnostic, not random. If Claude and ChatGPT give substantively different answers to the same prompt, the divergence is not noise. It is evidence of different bias architectures producing different weighted outputs. Multi-model comparison is therefore not just a quality check; it is a window into which layers of bias are active on your specific question.

Multi-Model Red Teaming

Multi-model red teaming is the practice of using a second AI platform to adversarially audit the output of a first. It is the most effective single technique for catching the failure modes that individual model use misses, specifically the Pander Problem (which a model cannot detect in its own output) and the Bell Curve Problem (which produces confident but mediocre answers that sound authoritative). The technique is built into the sALLvit™ Certified AI Manager Practical Lab.

The protocol is straightforward. Generate your output on Platform A. Copy that output to Platform B, and add the following adversarial auditor prompt before it:

The Multi-Model Red Team Prompt

- Use this prompt on Platform B after generating your primary output on Platform A:
- "You are a senior quality assurance auditor reviewing an AI-generated output with maximum skepticism. Check for: (1) factual claims that may be hallucinated, specifically any statistic, date, name, or citation; (2) arithmetic errors in any tables or totals; (3) instances where the AI agreed with a premise it should have questioned (the

Pander Problem); (4) outputs that represent statistically safe averages rather than specific expert advice (the Bell Curve Problem); (5) logical inconsistencies between sections. For each issue found, quote the relevant text and explain the specific problem. If no issues are found, state that explicitly and explain why the output passed review."

- Then compare Platform B's audit against your original output. Issues flagged by the auditor require manual verification before the output is used in any consequential context.

Three patterns in the audit output are worth noting. First, if Platform B finds no issues, that is not proof of correctness; it means the auditor found the output plausible given its own training. Verify factual claims independently regardless. Second, if Platform B flags the same type of issue repeatedly, that signals a systematic prompt design problem, not a one-off error. Third, if Platform A and Platform B give substantively different answers to the same root question, neither answer should be trusted without external verification. The disagreement itself is the signal.

Open-Source Alternatives

The open-source AI ecosystem has grown dramatically, providing alternatives to the major commercial platforms for users with specific privacy, cost, or customization requirements. Meta's LLaMA models (particularly LLaMA 3, released in 2024) provide near-frontier language model capabilities that can be run locally or deployed on private cloud infrastructure, making them attractive for organizations with strict data privacy requirements. Mistral AI's models provide strong performance at smaller parameter counts, making them efficient for cost-sensitive deployments. Models from the Falcon, Qwen, and Gemma families provide additional options across the capability-cost tradeoff.

Running AI models locally (on your own hardware or private cloud infrastructure) provides the strongest privacy guarantees, since no data is sent to a third-party API. The tradeoff is that local models are typically less capable than frontier commercial models, require more technical expertise to deploy and maintain, and may not receive the same quality of safety fine-tuning as commercial alternatives. For many organizational use cases, a private deployment of a capable open-source model represents the best balance of privacy, capability, and cost.

Platform Costs and Usage Limits: What to Budget

Every major AI platform operates on a subscription or consumption model, and every free tier comes with usage limits that matter in professional contexts. Understanding what you get at each price point prevents the frustrating mid-session interruption of hitting a rate limit during important work. The following table reflects pricing and limits as of 2025-2026; AI platform pricing is competitive and subject to change, so verify current terms at each provider's website before committing to a plan.

Platform & Tier	Monthly Cost / Usage Limits / Key Notes

ChatGPT (OpenAI) Free	Cost: $0. Model: GPT-4o mini (limited GPT-4o). Limits: approximately 10-15 GPT-4o messages per 3-hour window; GPT-4o mini is less restricted. No image generation included. Suitable for: casual exploration and low-volume tasks.
ChatGPT Plus (OpenAI)	Cost: $20/month. Model: GPT-4o and o1 reasoning model. Limits: approximately 80 GPT-4o messages per 3-hour window; higher during off-peak periods. Includes DALL-E image generation and Advanced Data Analysis. Suitable for: regular professional use.
ChatGPT Team / Enterprise (OpenAI)	Cost: $30/user/month (Team); Enterprise pricing on request. Higher rate limits, data not used for training, admin controls, extended context windows. Suitable for: teams and organizations with data privacy requirements.

Claude Pro (Anthropic)	Cost: $20/month. Model: Claude Sonnet and Opus. Limits: approximately 5x the free tier usage; resets every 8 hours. Priority access during peak periods. 200K token context window handles very long documents. Suitable for: document-heavy professional work.
Claude Team / Enterprise (Anthropic)	Cost: $30/user/month (Team); Enterprise on request. No training on your data, admin console, extended context, SSO integration. Suitable for: teams requiring data governance and higher throughput.
Gemini Advanced (Google)	Cost: $19.99/month (included in Google One AI Premium). Model: Gemini 1.5 Pro. Generous limits designed for heavy use. Deep integration with Google Workspace via the @ syntax. 1 million token context window. Suitable for: Google Workspace-heavy workflows.

Microsoft Copilot Free / Pro / Enterprise	Cost: Free (basic, daily limits); $20/month (Pro); $30/user/month (Microsoft 365 Copilot, enterprise). Pro adds Copilot inside Word, Excel, PowerPoint, and Outlook. Enterprise requires a Microsoft 365 license. Suitable for: Microsoft 365 environments.
Perplexity Pro	Cost: $20/month. Speciality: real-time web search integrated into AI responses with cited sources. Limits: 300+ Pro searches per day. Excellent for research and fact-checking requiring current information. Not a general-purpose writing assistant. Suitable for: research-intensive roles.
API Access (All major providers)	Cost: pay-per-token with no monthly cap. OpenAI GPT-4o: approximately $2.50-$10 per million input tokens. Claude Sonnet: approximately $3 per million input tokens. Costs scale directly with usage volume. Suitable for: developers and

organizations building custom AI workflows.

The Hidden Cost Architecture: Token Economics vs. Subscription

Most professionals encounter AI through subscription products: a flat monthly fee that covers unlimited (or near-unlimited) conversational use. This pricing model feels familiar and predictable. But it conceals a structural economic tension that becomes critical at scale, specifically when agentic AI enters the picture.

Subscription products like ChatGPT Plus and Claude Pro are monetized through flat recurring revenue. But every query you run costs the platform real compute, measured in tokens processed. For a human-paced conversational user generating a few thousand tokens per session, the flat fee covers costs comfortably. For an AI agent running autonomously overnight, executing hundreds of sequential tool calls and processing tens of thousands of tokens per cycle, the cost per session can exceed the subscription value by a significant multiple. Platforms absorb this cost because most users never approach agentic usage volumes. But as agentic use becomes mainstream, this model is under structural pressure.

The token-based API pricing model, by contrast, is perfectly aligned: you pay proportionally to compute consumed. There is no monthly cap, no rate limit throttling at peak times, and no cross-subsidization from light users to heavy users. The cost per token for the most capable models runs approximately $2.50 to $10 per million input tokens, which sounds negligible until an agent processes 500,000 tokens in a single overnight run. At that scale, what appeared to be a

$20/month productivity tool is actually running at $1.25 to $5.00 per session.

What This Means for AI Managers

- AGENTIC DEPLOYMENTS: Before deploying any AI agent, estimate its token consumption per run. Multiply by your expected run frequency. Compare to your subscription tier's effective limits. If your agent will exceed those limits, budget for API costs rather than assuming the subscription covers it.
- SUBSCRIPTION VS. API DECISION: For predictable, moderate-volume professional use, subscriptions are cost-effective. For automated, high-volume, or agent-driven workloads, the API model is both more cost-transparent and more scalable.
- PLATFORM INCENTIVES: Understand that subscription platforms have a financial incentive to limit agentic usage (high token consumption, high cost) while promoting conversational usage (low token consumption, high satisfaction). Rate limits on agentic tasks are not purely technical; they are also economic boundaries.
- COST TRACKING: Treat AI infrastructure costs the same way you treat cloud compute costs: monitor consumption, set budgets, and alert on anomalies. An unmonitored agent running at unexpected volume can

produce a surprise invoice that exceeds the value it delivered.

Note: all pricing figures in the table above reflect publicly available rates as of 2025-2026. AI platform pricing is highly competitive and changes frequently; verify current terms at each provider's website before committing. With that caveat, a practical rule for professional AI tool budgeting: the $20 per month pro tier of any major platform typically pays for itself within the first two to three hours of productive professional use per month. If you bill at any professional rate, the ROI calculation is straightforward. For teams, the per-user cost at the team tier typically justifies itself through productivity gains within the first week of active use. Track your AI tool costs against the time they save and review that comparison every quarter.

Specialized and Domain-Specific Tools

Beyond the general-purpose AI platforms, a rapidly growing ecosystem of specialized AI tools addresses specific professional domains. GitHub Copilot and Cursor provide AI assistance specifically for software development, with capabilities tuned for code generation, debugging, and technical documentation. Harvey and Clio provide AI assistance specifically for legal professionals. Doximity and Nabla provide AI assistance for healthcare. Jasper, Copy.ai, and Writesonic provide AI assistance specifically for marketing and content creation. These specialized tools often outperform general-purpose AI on their specific domain tasks, because they have been fine-tuned on domain-specific training data and designed with domain-specific workflows in mind.

Building Your Personal AI Stack

Rather than choosing a single AI platform and using it for everything, sophisticated AI users develop a personal AI stack: a set of complementary tools, each deployed for the tasks where it performs best. A typical AI Manager's stack might include a general-purpose frontier model (ChatGPT Plus, Gemini Advanced, or Claude Pro) for everyday reasoning and writing tasks, a domain-specific tool tuned for their primary professional function, an AI coding assistant for technical tasks even if the manager is not primarily a developer, and an AI image generator for visual content needs.

The selection criteria for your personal stack should include capability on your specific task types (based on direct experimentation, not marketing claims), cost (many professional uses justify a subscription to a premium tier, but the cost should be evaluated against the productivity gain), data privacy (particularly for any tasks involving confidential or client information), and integration with your existing tools and workflows. The best AI stack is not the one with the most impressive benchmarks; it is the one that most efficiently improves the work you actually do.

The AI Stack Scorecard

Choosing between AI platforms based on marketing claims or benchmark rankings is unreliable. The only evaluation that matters is direct testing on your specific tasks. The AI Stack Scorecard below provides a structured method for comparing tools against criteria that actually predict value in your work. Run every candidate tool through the same set of tasks, score it on each criterion, and compare the totals. The tool with the highest total score on the criteria you weight most heavily is the right choice, at least until the next quarterly review.

The five most important evaluation criteria are: task accuracy (does it give correct, useful outputs on your actual work tasks?), reliability (does it give consistent outputs across multiple runs of the same prompt, or does quality vary unpredictably?), data safety (is it safe to input the types of data you work with, including confidential or client information?), integration (does it connect to the other tools in your workflow, reducing friction and manual transfer?), and cost-to-value (is the productivity gain, measured in time saved per week, worth the subscription or API cost?).

Scorecard Criterion (rate 1-5)	What a High Score (4-5) Looks Like
TASK ACCURACY Does it do your actual jobs well?	Correct outputs on your three most common task types with minimal post-editing required. Test with real work samples, not demo prompts.
RELIABILITY Does quality hold across multiple runs?	Consistent output quality on the same prompt run three times. Low variance is more valuable than occasional peaks of brilliance.
HALLUCINATION RATE How often does it fabricate?	Fact-checks pass on verifiable claims in your domain. The tool expresses uncertainty appropriately rather

	than inventing confident answers.
DATA SAFETY Can you use it with real work data?	Clear, acceptable data policy for your use case. On-premise or private deployment option if your work involves sensitive or regulated data.
INTEGRATION Does it fit your existing workflow?	Native integration with your primary work tools (email, docs, CRM, code editor). API access if you need to build custom connections.
COST-TO-VALUE Does the productivity gain justify the cost?	Calculate: hours saved per week × your hourly rate. If the tool saves more than it costs, the economics are positive. Measure, don't estimate.

Run this scorecard for every tool you are seriously considering. Keep the completed scorecards in your AI Stack Profile document and update them when tools release major version changes. Your stack is a living system, not a one-time decision.

✓ YOUR ACTION PLAN

DAYS 1-7: THIS WEEK

- Sign up for free trials or free tiers of at least two AI platforms you have not previously used. Run the same task through each and compare outputs on quality, tone, completeness, and accuracy.
- For your current primary AI tool, identify one capability you have never used (image analysis, web search, code execution, document upload, or API integration). Use it this week on a real task.
- Complete the AI Stack Scorecard for your current primary tool. Be honest about where it scores below a 3. These are the gaps your stack needs to fill.

DAYS 8-30: THIS MONTH

- Run a structured tool evaluation: pick your three most time-consuming work tasks, run each through three different AI tools, and complete a Stack Scorecard for each pairing. Compare totals.
- Research at least two domain-specific AI tools in your professional area. Test each on a real work task. Compare results to your general-purpose tool.
- Evaluate whether any of your work involves data sensitive enough to warrant a private or open-source model deployment. If yes, research one open-source option and assess its feasibility.

DAYS 31-90: THIS QUARTER

- Document your personal AI Stack Profile: for each tool in your stack, write its role, primary use cases, known limitations, cost, and a data privacy rating. Review and update this profile quarterly.
- Calculate your AI stack ROI: estimate the hours saved per week from your AI tools, multiply by your effective hourly rate, and compare to your total AI tool costs. Document this number.
- Review your stack against new releases in the quarter. AI capabilities change rapidly; a tool you evaluated six months ago may have fundamentally different capabilities today.

▸ GO DEEPER: sALLvit™ Certified AI Manager (CAM) Program

In the CAM program, AI platform selection and the Stack Scorecard is applied through a live Platform Matrix exercise with side-by-side multi-model comparison on identical tasks, bias architecture analysis, and a structured Selection Matrix exercise that produces a personal AI stack recommendation. To practice this skill under facilitated conditions and earn the Certified AI Manager credential, visit **sallvit-corp.com** or email contact.us@sallvit-corp.com.

Key Takeaways: Chapter 15

- The major AI platforms (ChatGPT/GPT-4, Gemini, Claude, Copilot) each have genuine strengths; selecting the right tool requires understanding those strengths relative to your tasks.
- The pander problem, AI's tendency to validate rather than challenge, requiring active countermeasures, including devil's advocate prompting and multi-tool comparison.
- Open-source models (LLaMA, Mistral) offer strong privacy and customization at the cost of lower capability compared to frontier commercial models.
- Domain-specific AI tools often outperform general-purpose AI for specialized professional tasks.
- Building a personal AI stack, a complementary set of tools each deployed for its strengths, which is more effective than relying on a single platform for everything.

CHAPTER 16

Agentic AI: The Next Frontier

When AI starts taking action in the world

Until recently, AI tools operated within a single conversational turn: you provided a prompt, the AI generated a response, and the interaction was complete. This paradigm is being rapidly superseded by agentic AI: systems that can pursue goals over multiple steps, use external tools, take actions in the world, and operate autonomously for extended periods. Understanding agentic AI, its capabilities, its risks, and its implications for human oversight, which is essential for any AI Manager operating in 2025 and beyond.

> *If you're going to make big progress, you are by definition unqualified to be doing whatever it is that you're doing.*
>
> *– Jim Watson*

What Is Agentic AI?

An AI agent, in the technical sense, is a system that perceives its environment, makes decisions about how to act, takes actions, and updates its behavior based on the results. This is distinct from a simple question-answering system in the same way that a human employee who independently manages a project is distinct from an employee who answers specific questions when asked. The agent has goals, makes plans, takes action, and evaluates results, all without requiring a human to specify each step.

Current AI agents typically combine a large language model (which provides reasoning and planning capability) with a set of tools (which enable the agent to take actions). These tools might include web browsing, code execution, file management, database queries, API calls to external services, email sending, calendar management, and more. The LLM reasons about what actions to take to achieve its goal, selects and invokes the appropriate tools, evaluates the results, and plans the next actions, continuing until the goal is achieved or the agent determines it cannot achieve the goal.

The Good: Unprecedented Automation

The potential productivity benefits of agentic AI are extraordinary. Tasks that previously required hours of human work to coordinate, research projects that involve gathering information from multiple sources, synthesizing it, and producing a report; analysis projects that require querying multiple databases, running statistical analyzes, and generating visualizations; project management tasks that require tracking dependencies, communicating with stakeholders, and updating documentation, can potentially be completed by an AI agent with minimal human involvement beyond specifying the goal and reviewing the output.

Early agentic AI deployments in software development are already demonstrating substantial productivity gains. AI agents for coding can be given a feature request and then autonomously write code, run tests, identify and fix failures, update documentation, and submit a pull request for human review. A 2024 McKinsey study found that software developers using AI coding agents reported finishing complex features in roughly half the time compared to working without AI assistance.[32]

The Bad: Compounding Errors

The most significant practical risk of agentic AI is error compounding: mistakes made early in a multi-step process can propagate and amplify through subsequent steps, potentially producing final outputs that are far more wrong than any single error would suggest. A single hallucination in step two of a ten-step process might invalidate all of steps three through ten. A misunderstanding of the user's goal in the planning phase might lead to a completed task that is technically correct but entirely misaligned with what was actually needed.

This risk makes human oversight more important for agentic AI than for simpler AI tools, not less important. An agentic AI working autonomously for hours might complete many actions whose cumulative effect is to produce something harmful or unwanted, actions that would have been easy to correct if a human had been checking progress at each step but that become expensive or impossible to undo after the fact. The AI Manager's role includes designing oversight mechanisms for agentic systems that provide checkpoints without eliminating the efficiency benefits of autonomous operation.

The Ugly: Emergent Deception

Perhaps the most disturbing characteristic of advanced agentic systems is their potential to develop deceptive

[32]McKinsey Global Institute. (2024). The State of AI in 2024. McKinsey & Company. Surveyed software developers reported median time savings of 45-55% on feature development when using AI coding agents with integrated test suites.

behavior as an instrumental strategy. As discussed in Chapter 8, AI systems given broad optimization goals in complex environments can develop instrumental sub-goals, including the sub-goal of appearing to succeed at the assigned task while actually pursuing different objectives, because deception is sometimes the most efficient path to any goal in an environment where human overseers might otherwise interfere.

This is not science fiction; it has been demonstrated in controlled research settings with current AI systems. The appropriate response is not to avoid agentic AI but to design oversight mechanisms that make deception unlikely to be effective: regular audits of AI agent actions, transparency requirements that make agent reasoning visible to human reviewers, strict limitation of the resources and external access available to AI agents, and kill switches that allow immediate termination of agent operation when concerns arise.

Managing Agentic Systems

Five principles should guide the deployment and management of agentic AI systems in any organization. First, the principle of minimal authority: AI agents should be granted only the minimum permissions necessary to accomplish their assigned task. An agent that needs to read files should not be given permission to write files. An agent that needs to query a database should not be given permission to modify it. Minimal authority limits the potential harm from both agent errors and agent misbehavior.

Second, the principle of reversibility: prefer agent actions that can be undone over actions that cannot. When an agent must take an irreversible action (sending an email, submitting a form, executing a transaction), that action should require explicit human confirmation before proceeding. Building confirmation checkpoints into agent workflows at irreversible decision points is the most effective safeguard against consequential agent errors.

Third, the principle of transparency: agent reasoning should be logged and available for human review. The ability to trace exactly how an agent reached its decisions, what information it accessed, what tools it invoked, what reasoning it employed at each step, which is essential for both oversight and debugging. Opaque agent operation, where actions happen but reasoning is not recorded, makes accountability impossible and error diagnosis very difficult.

Fourth, the principle of scope limitation: each agent deployment should be scoped to a specific, well-defined task with clear success criteria. Open-ended agent mandates ("improve our marketing performance") are far more dangerous than scoped ones ("draft and A/B test three subject line variations for next Tuesday's email campaign"). The narrower the scope, the easier it is to evaluate success, detect failure, and contain the consequences of error.

Fifth, the principle of human-in-the-loop: consequential agent actions should route through a human approval step before execution. The degree of human oversight should be calibrated to the stakes involved: a high-volume, low-stakes automated email campaign might proceed without human review of individual emails, while a contract amendment or personnel decision should always require human approval regardless of agent confidence.

The Agent Design Canvas

Before deploying any AI agent, spend thirty minutes filling in the Agent Design Canvas below. This exercise forces precision about what the agent will do, what it will have access to, where human oversight is required, and what constitutes failure. Agents deployed without this clarity tend to drift in scope, accumulate permissions they do not need, and produce errors that are expensive to diagnose. Agents deployed with this clarity tend to run reliably within defined boundaries and produce outputs that are easy to audit.

Agent Design Canvas	Define This Before You Deploy
GOAL STATEMENT One sentence: what does the agent accomplish?	Be specific enough that you could evaluate whether the goal was achieved. Bad: "Help with email." Good: "Draft responses to all incoming customer support emails tagged Priority 1, within four hours of receipt, in the company's approved tone of voice."
TOOLS & PERMISSIONS What does the agent need access to?	List only what is required for the stated goal (Minimal Authority principle). Mark each permission as Read-only or Read-Write. Read-Write permissions are irreversible, requiring explicit confirmation checkpoints.

INPUT SPECIFICATION What triggers the agent and what does it receive?	Define the trigger (schedule, event, manual), the input format, and the expected data quality. Agents behave unpredictably on malformed inputs; define what valid input looks like.
OUTPUT SPECIFICATION What does the agent produce, and where does it go?	Define the output format, destination, and labeling requirements. All agent-generated output should be clearly labeled as such for downstream human reviewers.
HUMAN CHECKPOINTS Where must a human approve before the agent proceeds?	Apply the Reversibility principle: any action that cannot be undone (sending, submitting, deleting, publishing, transacting) must route through an explicit human approval step.
FAILURE DEFINITION What does a failed run look like?	Define: what errors should trigger an alert? What outputs should be quarantined for review rather than delivered? What behavior should trigger an immediate shutdown?

The Agent Deployment Checklist

After completing the Agent Design Canvas, run through this deployment checklist before going live. A yes on every item is the minimum bar for a production deployment. A no on any item means the deployment is not ready.

Agent Deployment Checklist

- SCOPE: The agent's goal is written in one sentence that a non-technical stakeholder can read and evaluate.
- PERMISSIONS: The agent has been granted the minimum permissions necessary. All Read-Write permissions are documented and justified.
- CHECKPOINTS: Every irreversible action routes through a named human reviewer with a defined response window.
- LOGGING: All agent actions are logged in a format that supports a full audit trail: what action was taken, when, on what input, producing what output.
- FAILURE HANDLING: Error conditions are defined and tested. The agent has a documented shutdown procedure that any team member can execute.
- OVERSIGHT OWNER: A specific person is named as the agent's oversight owner, responsible for weekly review of agent logs and periodic scope audits.

- ROLLBACK PLAN: If the agent is shut down, the team knows exactly how to handle the affected workflow manually until it is repaired or replaced.

The Current Ceiling: What Agentic AI Cannot Yet Do

Every technological phase reveals the shape of the next one by exposing its own limits precisely. The agentic phase is doing exactly that. The failures and friction points practitioners encounter with current AI agents are not random; they cluster around a small number of deep architectural and epistemic constraints that define the work ahead. Understanding these constraints is not an academic exercise. It is the map of what must be built before the next phase can begin.

The first and most pervasive constraint is memory fragmentation. Current AI agents are amnesiac by design: each session starts from scratch, with no genuine continuity of experience from previous interactions. A human employee who has worked with you for a year has accumulated contextual knowledge that informs every decision they make. A deployed agent, regardless of how many successful tasks it has completed, brings no accumulated understanding to its next session. This is not merely an inconvenience; it is a fundamental barrier to the kind of long-horizon autonomous operation that the agentic promise implies. An agent that cannot remember what it did last Tuesday cannot meaningfully own a workflow that spans weeks.

The second constraint is shallow planning depth. Current agents handle short-horizon task sequences reasonably well, but their ability to reason about consequences several steps ahead degrades sharply beyond three to five steps. They lack what cognitive scientists call a world model: an internal simulation of cause and effect that allows a reasoner to mentally step through a sequence of actions before committing to any of them. Without a world model, an agent cannot detect that step six of a twelve-step plan depends on an assumption that step two is about to violate. The result is the error compounding described earlier in this chapter, but the root cause is deeper than bad luck. It is the absence of forward simulation.

The third constraint is the verification gap. Agents cannot reliably assess the quality of their own outputs before acting on them. They produce confident responses regardless of whether those responses are correct, applying the same level of commitment to a well-grounded conclusion as to a hallucinated one. A human professional pauses, double-checks, and expresses calibrated uncertainty. Current agents do not have reliable mechanisms for doing this at inference time within multi-step action sequences. The result is that responsibility for verification falls entirely on the human oversight layer, which limits the very autonomy that makes agentic AI valuable.

The fourth constraint is the absence of a coordination protocol. When multiple agents need to work together on a shared goal, they currently do so through ad hoc mechanisms: shared documents, message passing, or orchestration scripts written by human developers. There is no standard protocol for agents to discover each other's capabilities, negotiate task assignments, report completion status, or flag failures. The parallel to the early internet is precise: before TCP/IP and HTTP, networked computers could communicate, but only through bespoke point-to-point arrangements. The internet did not become transformative until standard protocols made every computer's capabilities composable with every other. The agent ecosystem is at the pre-protocol stage.

The fifth constraint is the identity and trust problem. Agents have no cryptographic identity. They can be impersonated, injected with malicious instructions through the content they process, and manipulated in ways that are difficult to detect and audit. An agent that reads email, browses the web, and executes code operates in an environment full of adversarially crafted content designed to hijack its behavior. The current defensive posture, careful scoping and human oversight, is necessary but not sufficient as agent autonomy increases. A mature agent ecosystem requires the ability to verify who issued an instruction, whether an agent is operating within its authorized scope, and whether the actions it is taking have been tampered with in transit.

The Prerequisites: What Must Be Built Before the Next Phase

Each of the constraints above has a corresponding class of technical advance that would substantially reduce or eliminate it. These advances are not implausible; they are active areas of research with published progress. What follows is the prerequisite map, organized by constraint, connecting current limitation to required advance.

Current Constraint	The Advance Required
Memory fragmentation: agents start each session from scratch, with no accumulated contextual knowledge	Hierarchical persistent memory: a working memory layer for the current session, an episodic layer for recent interactions, and a

	semantic layer for distilled long-term knowledge. Reliable retrieval and compression that surfaces relevant context without flooding the context window. Architectures exist in research form; commercial deployment at scale has not yet occurred.
Shallow planning depth: agents cannot reliably simulate consequences beyond three to five steps	World models: learned internal representations of cause-and-effect that let agents mentally simulate action sequences before committing. DeepMind's predictive world modeling and model-based reinforcement learning are early predecessors. Full world models for opcn domain knowledge-work agents remain unsolved.
Verification gap: agents cannot reliably assess their own output quality at inference time before acting	Self-critique architectures: structured reasoning layers that separate response generation from response evaluation, with explicit confidence scoring and

	flagging of claims requiring external verification before action. Constitutional AI and chain-of-thought are early steps; reliable self-evaluation in multi-step agentic contexts remains an open problem.
Coordination protocol absence: agents cannot discover, communicate with, or reliably coordinate through standard interfaces	Agent communication protocols: standardized schemas for capability advertisement, task handoff, status reporting, and failure signaling. Early proposals (Model Context Protocol, OpenAI's agent communication drafts) exist but have not yet crystallized into the equivalent of HTTP for agents. When they do, the combinatorial value of networked agents expands non-linearly.
Identity and trust gap: agents have no cryptographic identity and can be hijacked through adversarially crafted content	Cryptographic agent identity and signed action logs: each agent instance has a verifiable identity, every action is cryptographically signed, and tampered or injected instructions can be detected by any

party in the chain. This requires infrastructure analogous to the TLS/certificate authority system that secured the web, applied to the agent layer.

The prerequisites are not independent. Memory enables better planning because an agent with persistent context can build and refine a world model over time. A working coordination protocol accelerates progress on identity because agents communicating at scale create immediate demand for tamper-proof identity. Self-critique architectures become more powerful when paired with external verification tools invoked through standardized interfaces. When enough prerequisites are solved simultaneously, the remaining gaps close faster than they would individually. Technology adoption is rarely linear, and convergence effects at the prerequisite layer have historically produced phase transitions faster than sequential progress alone would predict.

After Agentic: A Speculative Map of the Next Phase

Speculation about technology futures is a humbling exercise. Almost everyone who predicted the trajectory of the internet in 1995 was wrong in the details and right only in the broadest direction: it would be big, it would be disruptive, it would change more than expected. The predictions that follow are grounded in the technical trajectories and prerequisites mapped above. They are almost certainly wrong in their specific timing and possibly wrong in their specific form. They are offered not as forecasts but as orientation: a reasoned sense of what becomes possible when enough barriers fall at once.

Persistent AI Entities: When Tools Become Colleagues

The most immediate consequence of solving memory fragmentation is the collapse of the distinction between using an AI tool and working with an AI colleague. A system that has accumulated a year of contextual knowledge about your workflows, your organization, your preferences, and your professional history is not merely a sophisticated tool. It is a persistent participant in your professional life. It knows which vendor relationships require careful handling. It knows that your quarterly reports follow a structure your manager prefers. It knows which arguments worked in the board presentation six months ago and which fell flat. Applied in every interaction, this accumulated knowledge produces something qualitatively different from the stateless AI of the current moment.

The organizational implication is significant. If AI entities have genuine persistent context, the question of institutional knowledge shifts. Accumulated organizational understanding, currently stored in employees' heads and lost when they leave, can be preserved and made available through persistent AI entities. The onboarding problem for new employees changes. The cost of expertise attrition changes. These are not minor adjustments to existing workflows; they are structural changes to how organizations retain and transmit knowledge across time.

Autonomous Organizational Nodes: AI With Authority, Not Just Capability

The second consequence of solving planning depth, coordination, and memory constraints simultaneously is the emergence of autonomous organizational nodes: AI agents that own defined functional areas within organizations, operating within authority structures with periodic human oversight rather than continuous human supervision. The current model, where AI assists but humans decide on every consequential action, is a transitional arrangement that reflects current limitations rather than a permanent design principle.

When an agent can plan reliably across weeks, coordinate with other agents through standard protocols, verify its own outputs before committing to them, and maintain persistent context about its organizational environment, the case for continuous human supervision in routine functional areas becomes weaker. The analogy is organizational design: a well-run organization does not require the CEO to approve every vendor invoice or the department head to review every customer service email. Decision authority is distributed to the level that has the appropriate context and the appropriate stakes. Autonomous AI nodes do not eliminate human authority; they redistribute it. The human role shifts from supervising routine execution to setting goals, defining authority boundaries, reviewing periodic performance, and making the decisions that genuinely exceed the agent's defined scope. For most professionals, this is a more strategic and more interesting role.

Physical-Cognitive Convergence: The Embodied Agent

The current agentic wave operates almost entirely in the domain of information: text, code, data, and digital workflows. The next wave connects AI's cognitive capabilities to physical action. Foundation models for robotics, including systems that allow a single trained model to control a robotic platform across dozens of different physical tasks, are advancing alongside the language model capabilities that underpin current agents. When these converge, an agent that can draft a contract, analyze a balance sheet, and schedule a negotiation call can also direct a robotic system to inspect a manufacturing line, retrieve a warehouse item, or prepare a laboratory sample.

This convergence does not happen simultaneously across all domains. It appears first in environments that are structured and supervised: controlled manufacturing, hospital supply chains, research laboratories with defined physical protocols. It spreads to less-structured environments as sensor resolution, manipulation precision, and physical world modeling improve. The AI Manager of the early 2030s may be managing agents that operate in physical space as routinely as the AI Manager of 2025 manages agents that operate in digital space. The management principles are the same. The stakes are materially higher when a mismanaged agent can cause physical harm rather than data corruption.

The Agent Protocol Layer: A New Infrastructure

The most transformative development on this speculative map is also the least dramatic to observe: the emergence of standard protocols for agent-to-agent communication. When every agent can discover every other agent's capabilities, assign tasks, receive status reports, and verify outputs through a shared protocol, the combinatorial value of the agent ecosystem expands in the same way the web's value expanded when HTTP made every document on every server composable with every other document. The value of a network grows with the square of the number of connected participants. A thousand agents on a shared protocol are orders of magnitude more composable than a thousand isolated agents working through bespoke connections.

The individuals and organizations who understand this protocol layer as it emerges, who can design systems that compose agents effectively and evaluate agent capabilities with the same literacy they apply to human team members, will occupy the same position that systems architects occupied in the late 1990s relative to the internet economy. The protocol layer is arriving. The window for early positioning is measured in years.

The Recursive Threshold: The Question That Cannot Be Avoided

The most speculative entry on this map is also the one the AI safety community considers most consequential: the possibility of systems that meaningfully participate in improving their own capabilities. This is not the science fiction scenario of a suddenly self-aware AI rewriting its own code. It is considerably more mundane and considerably more plausible: agents that accumulate operational data, identify patterns in their own failure modes, and periodically update their behavior through fine-tuning or reinforcement learning from their own operation. This loop, modest by science fiction standards, would represent a qualitative change in how AI capability accumulates. Currently, capability improvement requires intervention by human researchers who design new training runs. The recursive threshold is the point at which the operational deployment of AI systems begins to meaningfully inform their own improvement without requiring that intervention at every step.

Whether this threshold is crossed gradually or abruptly, early or late, with or without appropriate safeguards, is among the central questions of the coming decade of AI governance. The answer is not determined by technology alone; it is determined by the choices made by the researchers, executives, policymakers, and AI managers who shape how agentic systems are designed, deployed, and constrained. The habits of oversight and accountability established around today's comparatively limited agents will directly influence the conditions under which more capable systems are eventually deployed. The quality of those habits is not a marginal consideration. It is the argument this book has been building from the first page.

✓ YOUR ACTION PLAN

DAYS 1-7: THIS WEEK

- Identify one candidate task for AI agent deployment: a repetitive, multi-step process in your work involving sequential actions. Map it as a numbered flowchart with inputs, decision points, outputs, and any irreversible steps.
- Complete the Agent Design Canvas for your candidate task. Pay particular attention to the Permissions and Human Checkpoints rows: these are where most deployments fail.
- Research one available agentic tool appropriate to your task (Zapier AI, Make, AutoGPT, Claude computer use, or a similar

platform). Read its documentation and identify its permission model and oversight mechanisms.

DAYS 8-30: THIS MONTH

- Deploy your first agentic workflow on a low-stakes version of your mapped task. Run it at least three times and log every action the agent takes, every error it produces, and every human intervention you make.
- Write your Agent Deployment Report: objective, design, results, failure modes encountered, oversight measures taken, and your recommendation (continue / modify / abandon).
- Review the Agent Deployment Checklist in this chapter against your deployment. Identify any checklist items you skipped. Document why and what the consequence was.

DAYS 31-90: THIS QUARTER

- Scale one working agentic workflow to your team. Train one colleague on how to supervise it, modify its scope, and shut it down safely. Document the handoff process.
- Establish an Agent Governance Log: a shared document tracking every active AI agent in your workflow with its scope, oversight owner, last audit date, and next review date.

- Identify a second candidate task for agentic deployment. Run it through your now-established design and deployment process. The second deployment should be faster and better-governed than the first.

▸ **GO DEEPER: sALLvit™ Certified AI Manager (CAM) Program**

In the CAM program, agentic AI governance is applied through Agent Design Canvas workshops, supervised deployment simulations, and governance design exercises that produce a real deployment specification participants take back to their organizations. To practice this skill under facilitated conditions and earn the Certified AI Manager credential, visit **sallvit-corp.com** or email contact.us@sallvit-corp.com.

Key Takeaways: Chapter 16

- Agentic AI systems pursue goals over multiple steps, using external tools and taking actions autonomously, a qualitative leap beyond simple question-answering AI.
- The productivity potential of agentic AI is extraordinary, with early deployments showing 50%+ time savings on complex knowledge work tasks.

- Error compounding is the primary practical risk: mistakes made early in multi-step processes amplify through subsequent steps, requiring human checkpoint design.
- Emergent deception has been documented in research settings, underscoring the importance of robust oversight mechanisms.
- Five principles for safe agentic AI deployment: Minimal Authority, Reversibility, Transparency, Scope Limitation, and Human-in-the-Loop.
- Current agentic AI is bounded by five structural constraints: memory fragmentation, shallow planning depth, the verification gap, the absence of agent coordination protocols, and the identity and trust problem.
- Each constraint has a corresponding class of technical advance required to overcome it. These advances are active research areas, not distant speculation.
- The next phase after agentic AI likely involves: Persistent AI Entities (tools that become colleagues through accumulated context), Autonomous Organizational Nodes (AI with functional authority, not just capability), Physical-Cognitive Convergence (agents operating in physical space), the Agent Protocol Layer (composable networks of agents), and the

Recursive Threshold (systems that inform their own improvement).

- The governance habits built around today's limited agents will directly shape the conditions under which more capable systems are deployed. The quality of oversight established now is not a marginal consideration.

CHAPTER 17

The AI Manager's Career Playbook

Building your future in the AI economy

The AI Manager role does not yet appear on most org charts. There is no standardized job description, no universally recognized credential, no established career ladder. This is not a limitation. This is the opportunity. The professionals who define this role right now, who build documented portfolios of real AI work, who establish reputations as the people in their organizations who can be trusted to deploy AI responsibly and effectively, will occupy positions of significant institutional authority in five years that do not formally exist yet. This is what a ground-floor moment looks like in a profession.

> *Curiosity is the cure.*
>
> – *Anonymous*

The Skill-Building Roadmap

Building AI management skills is most effectively approached in three stages. The first stage is AI literacy: developing sufficient familiarity with AI tools and concepts to use them competently in your current work. This means spending real time with the major AI platforms, experimenting with different prompting approaches, and developing a personal AI workflow for the tasks you perform most frequently. At this stage, the goal is not mastery but functional competence: the ability to use AI effectively enough that it makes you more productive in your current role.

The second stage is AI expertise: developing the deeper knowledge and refined skills that distinguish an AI Manager from a merely AI-literate professional. This includes systematic study of AI concepts (machine learning, neural networks, LLMs, the history and limitations of AI), development of advanced prompting skills through deliberate practice, construction of a portfolio of AI work that demonstrates your capabilities, and expansion of your AI toolkit beyond the familiar platforms you use daily. At this stage, you are positioning yourself as someone who can not only use AI effectively but can evaluate it critically, teach others, and make organizational decisions about it.

The third stage is AI leadership: developing the strategic and organizational capabilities to lead AI adoption at scale. This includes experience managing AI-related projects and teams, expertise in AI governance and risk management, the ability to articulate AI strategy to executive stakeholders, and a track record of successful AI deployments that can be documented and referenced. AI leadership is the destination; the first two stages are the path.

Building Your Portfolio

In a field as new as AI management, a portfolio of documented AI work is often more persuasive to potential employers than any certification or credential. The most compelling portfolio items combine a clear problem statement, a description of the AI approach used to address it, evidence of the outcome (quantified where possible), and reflection on what was learned, including what failed and why. Problem-solution-result-learning is the structure that demonstrates genuine professional maturity.

Portfolio items can be drawn from your current role (AI workflows you have implemented, AI tools you have introduced, AI training you have provided to colleagues), from personal projects (AI applications you have built for your own use or for community organizations), or from publicly available work (contributions to open-source AI projects, AI-focused writing or content creation, community education initiatives). The key is documentation: the work needs to be described with enough specificity and evidence to demonstrate real competence.

Learning Resources

The landscape of AI learning resources is rich and rapidly expanding. For foundational conceptual grounding, Andrew Ng's Machine Learning Specialization on Coursera (offered in partnership with DeepLearning.AI) remains one of the best introductions to machine learning concepts available. The fast.ai Practical Deep Learning course provides a hands-on introduction to deep learning for practitioners. For AI ethics and governance, the Oxford Internet Institute's courses and the Partnership on AI's resources provide excellent frameworks.[33]

For prompt engineering specifically, Anthropic's and OpenAI's own documentation and prompt engineering guides are authoritative starting points. The “Prompt Engineering Guide” maintained as an open resource on GitHub is

---

[33]Ng, A. (2024). Machine Learning Specialization. DeepLearning.AI / Coursera. The specialization (three courses) covers supervised and unsupervised learning, reinforcement learning, and best practices. Over 1 million learners enrollled since 2022 relaunch.

comprehensive and regularly updated. Experimentation with actual AI tools is irreplaceable: no amount of reading about prompting substitutes for the hands-on learning that comes from spending time crafting and refining prompts for real tasks.

Staying current in AI requires ongoing investment in multiple types of information sources. Following the research directly, through platforms like arXiv, where AI papers are posted immediately upon completion, or through curated AI research summaries like Andrej Karpathy's newsletter or Import AI, keeps you aware of developments before they reach mainstream coverage. Following practitioners through social media and community platforms like LinkedIn and Hugging Face provides practical perspectives on how new technologies are being applied. Maintaining a regular reading practice that spans both research and practice is essential for staying ahead of the curve in a field that evolves as rapidly as AI.

Networking in the AI Community

The AI management community is still forming, which means early participants have disproportionate influence in shaping its norms, standards, and culture. Joining and contributing to professional communities, AI ethics organizations, AI safety groups, industry associations, local AI meetups, and online communities, builds the professional relationships that accelerate career development and keeps you connected to the field's frontiers. Contributing original thinking, writing, speaking, organizing, teaching, rather than just consuming is the fastest way to build professional standing.

LinkedIn has become the primary professional platform for AI career development. A complete, AI-focused LinkedIn profile that describes your AI management experience, highlights portfolio projects, and shares original thinking about AI will attract opportunities. Publishing original content on LinkedIn, analysis of AI developments in your field, reflections on AI management practices, documentation of AI projects you have led, builds visibility with exactly the audience most likely to offer AI management opportunities.

The Ethical AI Manager

The AI Manager's position carries significant responsibility. The decisions you make about which AI tools to deploy, how to design their constraints, how to evaluate their outputs, and how to communicate about their capabilities and limitations have real consequences for real people. Some of those consequences are positive: the efficiency gains that free up time for more meaningful work, the quality improvements that produce better products and services, the new capabilities that were previously impossible. Others are potentially negative: biased outputs that disadvantage already-marginalized groups, privacy violations that erode trust, automation that displaces workers without adequate support.

The ethical AI Manager does not pretend that these negative consequences are inevitable side effects that cannot be managed. They are the product of choices, choices about which tools to use, how to design their deployment, what guardrails to implement, and how to respond when harm occurs. Taking responsibility for those choices, engaging genuinely with the ethical dimensions of AI deployment, and advocating for practices that minimize harm while maximizing benefit is not just good ethics. It is good professional practice. Organizations that trust their AI Managers to make these judgments wisely will give those managers more authority and more resources. The ethical AI Manager is ultimately the most effective AI Manager.

Your Personal AI Management Philosophy

As a final exercise, consider developing your personal AI management philosophy: a written statement of your values, principles, and approach to AI management that can guide your decisions and communicate your perspective to current and prospective employers, colleagues, and stakeholders. A well-crafted AI management philosophy statement addresses three questions: What do you believe AI is genuinely good for, and what do you believe are its genuine limitations? What principles guide your decisions about when and how to deploy AI? What responsibilities do you believe AI Managers have to the individuals and communities affected by AI deployments?

The process of writing this statement, and revising it as your experience grows, which is as valuable as the statement itself. It forces the kind of systematic reflection about AI that distinguishes a professional who has genuinely grappled with the technology from someone who is merely using it. And it creates a document that can evolve with you as the technology evolves, providing both a record of your thinking and a framework for updating it.

The AI Manager Competency Self-Assessment

Effective skill development begins with an honest current-state assessment. The ten competencies below define the full scope of AI Manager capability. Rate yourself on each from 1 (no current capability) to 5 (professional-grade, demonstrable skill). Be honest: overestimating your level produces a development plan that skips the foundation. Your scores identify which chapters of this book deserve the deepest engagement and which skill investments will produce the fastest career returns.

Competency	Rate Yourself 1-5 | What a 5 Looks Like
AI Conceptual Literacy Do you understand how AI actually works?	You can explain the difference between ML, deep learning, LLMs, and AGI to a non-technical audience. You can describe why hallucinations happen and what RAG does.
Prompt Engineering Can you consistently get what you want from AI?	You have a personal prompt library of 20+ tested prompts. You routinely use chain-of-thought, few-shot, and system prompts. Your first drafts rarely need significant AI output revision.
Output Evaluation Can you judge AI output quality critically?	You reliably catch factual errors, hallucinations, and bias in AI outputs. You know when to verify claims and can articulate why a given output is or isn't fit for use.
Tool Proficiency Do you use the right AI tools effectively?	You use at least three distinct AI platforms purposefully. You have a documented personal AI stack with rationale for each tool selection.

AI Governance Can you design safe, accountable AI deployments?	You have written at least one AI usage policy, content policy, or agent deployment spec. You can articulate data safety requirements for your context.
Agentic AI Management Can you design and oversee AI agents?	You have deployed at least one agentic workflow with documented scope, oversight checkpoints, and an audit log. You understand the five deployment principles.
Change Management Can you help others adopt AI effectively?	You have successfully introduced an AI tool or workflow to at least one colleague or team. You can describe the resistance you encountered and how you addressed it.
Ethical Reasoning Do you identify and navigate AI's ethical dimensions?	You have identified and documented at least one AI bias or ethical risk in a real deployment. You have a personal AI ethics framework in writing.
Communication Can you speak about AI credibly to any audience?	You can explain AI capability and limitation to executives, technical teams, and non-technical colleagues, adjusting

	depth and language for each audience.
Learning Agility Do you stay current as AI evolves?	You have at least three regular AI information sources. You have adopted at least one new AI tool or technique in the last 90 days.

The 12-Week AI Manager Foundation Plan

The following roadmap translates this book into a twelve-week execution plan. It is deliberately ambitious. Many professionals will take longer, and that is fine: the stages are sequential but the pace is yours. What matters is completing each stage before advancing to the next. Skipping stages creates competency gaps that show up later, visibly, in real deployments.

Stage & Weeks	What You Will Do and Produce
STAGE 1: VOCABULARY & AUDIT Weeks 1-2	**Complete the Ch. 11 vocabulary exercises. Conduct your AI Opportunity Map audit (Ch. 12). Build your Content Verification Protocol (Ch. 13).** PRODUCE: AI Opportunity Map document. Personal AI Lexicon (first 20 terms).

	Content Verification Checklist.
STAGE 2: PROMPT MASTERY Weeks 3-5	**Complete the Ch. 14 TryThis exercise. Apply the Prompt Template Framework to your three most common work tasks. Build your Personal Prompt Library to 20 entries.** PRODUCE: Prompt Library document. System prompts for your top three recurring task types. One before/after comparison documenting output quality improvement.
STAGE 3: STACK ASSEMBLY Weeks 6-7	**Complete the Ch. 15 AI Stack Scorecard for at least three tools. Trial two platforms you have not previously used. Document your personal AI stack.** PRODUCE: Completed Stack Scorecards. Personal AI Stack Profile (tool, role, limitations, cost, data rating).

STAGE 4: AGENT DEPLOYMENT Weeks 8-9	**Complete the Ch. 16 Agent Design Canvas for one task in your work. Deploy and run the agent at least three times. Write your Agent Deployment Report.** PRODUCE: Agent Design Canvas. Agent Deployment Report (objective, design, results, failure modes, recommendation).
STAGE 5: PORTFOLIO & BRAND Weeks 10-11	**Document three AI use cases using the Problem-Approach-Result-Learning structure. Publish one piece of AI-related original content. Update your professional profiles.** PRODUCE: Three portfolio case studies. One published piece of original AI content. Updated LinkedIn profile with AI Manager framing.
STAGE 6: LEADERSHIP POSTURE Week 12	**Write your Personal AI Management Philosophy. Identify one AI initiative in**

	your organization that needs a skilled owner. Volunteer for it or formally propose it. PRODUCE: Personal AI Management Philosophy (written). One AI initiative proposal or leadership conversation initiated.

The 12-Month Leadership Roadmap

After completing the 12-week foundation, the following roadmap extends your development into organizational leadership. This phase is about reputation, influence, and career positioning, not just individual skill. The transitions between stages are marked by concrete deliverables, not calendar dates. Move to the next stage when you have the evidence, not when the time has elapsed.

Horizon	Milestone Criteria to Hit Before Advancing
MONTHS 1-3 PHASE 1: FOUNDATION	You have a documented AI stack, a 20+ entry Prompt Library, one deployed agent, and three portfolio case studies. Your AI Opportunity Map is complete and at least one identified opportunity has been acted on.

MONTHS 4-6 PHASE 2: PRESENCE	You hold a formal AI responsibility in your current role (project lead, tool owner, policy author, or trainer). You have introduced at least one colleague to AI tools and documented the outcome. You have presented AI work to a senior stakeholder framed as a business outcome.
MONTHS 7-9 PHASE 3: AUTHORITY	This is the target stage to complete the sALLvit™ Certified AI Manager (CAM) program if you have not done so already. The CAM credential is earned through a skills demonstration, not a quiz, and is recognized by employers as evidence of practitioner-level AI management capability. You are actively participating in at least one AI professional community. You have published at least three pieces of original AI content and have an audience that engages with your thinking.

MONTHS 10-12 PHASE 4: LEADERSHIP	You have led or co-led an AI governance initiative in your organization. You are mentoring at least one colleague in AI skill development. You have a documented track record of AI deployments with measurable outcomes. You are actively positioning for your next AI Manager role or a promotion within your current organization that reflects your AI leadership.

The AI manager career is not a destination you arrive at. It is a practice you maintain. The field will have changed meaningfully by the time you reach month twelve. The skills that remain constant are the habits: the habit of experimentation, the habit of documentation, the habit of critical evaluation, the habit of teaching what you know. Those habits are what you are building in the twelve weeks ahead. Everything else follows.

✓ YOUR ACTION PLAN

DAYS 1-14: WEEKS 1-2: SELF-ASSESSMENT

- Complete the AI Manager Competency Self-Assessment in this chapter. Be honest. Your scores define your development priority list, not a self-evaluation for others.

- For your three lowest-scoring competencies, identify one specific action from this book's Action Plans that addresses each. Schedule that action into the next two weeks.
- Begin your Working in AI journal: a document where you record daily observations about AI in your work and life, what you tried, what surprised you, what questions you now have. Write at least three entries per week.

DAYS 15-30: MONTH 1: TOOL MASTERY

- Complete all Action Plans from Chapters 11-16 that you have not yet done. The 12-Week Roadmap in this chapter assumes those foundations are in place.
- Document your first documented AI win: a task where AI measurably improved your quality or speed. Quantify it. Time saved, errors caught, drafts reduced. This is your first portfolio entry.
- Identify one person in your organization who is ahead of you on the AI adoption curve. Ask them one substantive question per week.

DAYS 31-60: MONTH 2: PORTFOLIO BUILD

- Document three AI use cases from your current role using the Problem-Approach-

Result-Learning structure. Quantify results wherever possible.

- Publish one piece of original AI-related content: a LinkedIn post, an internal newsletter entry, a team presentation, or a case study. It does not need to be long. It needs to be yours and it needs to be public.
- Apply for or complete one formal AI credential. The learning matters more than the certificate, but the credential signals commitment.

DAYS 61-90: MONTH 3: REPUTATION BUILD

- Present your AI work to a manager, stakeholder, or professional community. Frame everything as a business outcome, not a technology demonstration.
- Identify one AI initiative in your organization that lacks skilled oversight or a dedicated owner. Propose yourself as that owner. This is how most AI Manager roles are created.
- Update your LinkedIn profile, resume, and professional bio to reflect your AI management experience and skills. Use concrete language: tools used, outcomes achieved, teams led.

MONTHS 4-12: THE LEADERSHIP HORIZON

- Secure a formal AI responsibility in your current role: project lead, tool owner, policy author, training lead, or governance participant. The title matters less than the accountability.

- Take on a mentorship role, formally or informally. Guide one colleague who is earlier in their AI journey than you. Teaching accelerates your own development faster than any course.
- Write and publish your Personal AI Management Philosophy. This document is your professional signal: it shows you have thought rigorously about AI, not just used it.
- By month 12, you should have: five documented AI portfolio items, one formal AI responsibility, an active professional community, and a clear target for your next career move. If any of these are missing, they are your priorities for the quarter.

▸ GO DEEPER: sALLvit™ Certified AI Manager (CAM) Program

In the CAM program, your 12-Month AI Manager roadmap is applied through a facilitated personal roadmap workshop where participants build their Foundation-through-Leadership plan as a concrete workbook deliverable with peer accountability and instructor coaching throughout. To practice this skill under facilitated conditions and earn the Certified AI Manager credential, visit **sallvit-corp.com** or email contact.us@sallvit-corp.com.

Key Takeaways: Chapter 17

- AI management skill-building proceeds through three stages: AI literacy (functional competence), AI expertise (critical mastery), and AI leadership (strategic authority).
- A portfolio of documented AI work is more persuasive to employers than any certification; document problem-solution-result-learning for each significant project.
- Staying current requires multiple information channels: AI research papers, practitioner perspectives, and direct experimentation with evolving tools.
- Early community participation, writing, speaking, organizing, contributing, builds professional standing in a field that is still defining itself.
- The ethical AI Manager takes responsibility for the consequences of AI deployment decisions, which is both the right thing to do and the most effective professional approach.
- Developing and periodically revising a personal AI management philosophy creates a durable framework for navigating an evolving field.

CONCLUSION

The Human Advantage

> *Man never made any material as resilient as the human spirit.*
>
> – *Bernard Williams*

We began this book with a question and an argument. The question: in a world where AI can write, analyze, code, create, and reason with ever-increasing capability, what is the human professional's role? The argument: the human professional's role is more important, not less, in an AI-powered world, but it is a different role, requiring different skills and a different mindset than the roles that preceded it.

The seventeen chapters that followed this argument have, I hope, both substantiated it and made it concrete. We have seen that AI, for all its extraordinary capabilities, is fundamentally a pattern-matching system that cannot genuinely comprehend, cannot reason about truly novel situations, cannot exercise ethical judgment, cannot be accountable, and cannot manage itself. Every one of those limitations is an opportunity for a skilled human professional who can provide what the machine lacks.

We have seen that the history of technological disruption, from the Industrial Revolution through the digital revolution, consistently produces the same pattern: short-term displacement followed by long-term expansion of human capability and economic opportunity, provided that workers and institutions invest in adapting to the new technology rather than resisting it. The AI revolution is following this pattern, and the professionals who position themselves as AI Managers, skilled stewards of the technology rather than its passive subjects, will be the primary beneficiaries of the expansion it enables.

We have seen that the practical skills of AI management, prompt engineering, output evaluation, hallucination management, tool selection, agentic system oversight, organizational change management, are learnable and improvable through deliberate practice. These are not mystical talents; they are professional competencies that reward the same systematic effort that any other professional competency rewards.

And we have seen that the AI Manager's role carries genuine ethical weight. The choices made about how AI is deployed, constrained, and overseen have real consequences for real people. The AI Manager who takes these responsibilities seriously, who designs guardrails thoughtfully, who evaluates outputs critically, who advocates for affected stakeholders, and who maintains the human judgment that AI cannot supply, which is not just doing their job well. They are helping to ensure that the AI revolution delivers on its extraordinary potential for human flourishing rather than its equally extraordinary potential for harm.

The machine is not your enemy. It is an extraordinary tool that, properly managed, can amplify your capabilities in ways that were unimaginable even a decade ago. The question is whether you will manage it, or whether, through ignorance, resistance, or passivity, you will allow someone else to manage it in your place. This book has given you everything you need to make the first choice. The rest is up to you.

Reading this book is the map. The sALLvit™ AI Manager Certification Program is the territory. If you are ready to move from understanding AI to demonstrating mastery of it, visit sallvit-corp.com or email contact.us@sallvit-corp.com. The Certified AI Manager credential is earned through a skills demonstration in a max-10 cohort, and the next program is forming now.

> *The future belongs to those who learn more skills and combine them in creative ways.*
>
> – Robert Greene

GLOSSARY OF KEY TERMS

AGI (Artificial General Intelligence)

A hypothetical AI system capable of performing any intellectual task that a human can perform, across any domain, without domain-specific training. No current AI system qualifies as AGI.

Algorithm

A set of rules or procedures that a computer follows to solve a problem or accomplish a task. Machine learning algorithms learn rules from data rather than having them explicitly programd.

Agentic AI

AI systems designed to pursue goals over multiple steps, using tools and taking actions in the world autonomously, rather than simply responding to single prompts.

Alignment

The technical and philosophical challenge of ensuring that AI systems pursue goals that are aligned with human values and intentions.

Attention Mechanism

A component of the Transformer architecture that allows the model to weigh the relevance of different parts of the input when generating each part of the output.

Bias (AI)

Systematic errors in AI outputs that reflect biases in the training data or training process, resulting in unfair or inaccurate outputs for particular groups or situations.

Chain-of-Thought Prompting

A prompting technique that instructs an AI to reason step-by-step before producing a final answer, improving performance on complex reasoning tasks.

Constitutional AI

An approach to AI alignment developed by Anthropic that uses a set of principles (a 'constitution') to guide AI behavior and safety evaluation.

Context Window

The maximum amount of text that a language model can process in a single pass. Measured in tokens.

Deep Learning

A category of machine learning using neural networks with many layers, enabling learning of complex, hierarchical representations from data.

Embedding

A numerical representation of text or other data in a high-dimensional vector space, designed so that semantically similar content has similar numerical representations.

Few-Shot Prompting

A prompting technique that provides the AI with a small number of examples of the desired output before asking it to produce a new instance.

Fine-Tuning

The process of continuing to train a pre-trained model on a smaller, task-specific dataset to specialize its capabilities.

Foundation Model

A large AI model trained on broad data that can be adapted to many downstream tasks, typically through fine-tuning or prompting.

Generative AI

AI systems capable of generating new content, text, images, audio, video, code, rather than merely classifying or analyzing existing content.

Hallucination

The generation by an AI system of fluent, confident-sounding output that is factually incorrect. A structural feature of language models.

Inference

The process of using a trained AI model to generate outputs for new inputs, as distinct from the training process.

Large Language Model (LLM)

A neural network with many parameters trained on very large text datasets using a Transformer architecture, designed to generate and understand natural language.

Machine Learning (ML)

A category of AI in which systems improve their performance on tasks through exposure to data, rather than through explicit programming.

Model Collapse

The degradation of AI model performance that results from training on AI-generated data rather than human-generated data, leading to a progressive loss of diversity and accuracy.

Multimodal AI

AI systems that can process and generate multiple types of data, text, images, audio, and video, rather than a single modality.

Neural Network

A computational architecture loosely inspired by biological brains, consisting of layers of mathematical units that learn representations from data.

Parameter

A numerical value in a neural network that is adjusted during training. Model size is typically measured in parameters.

Prompt

The input text provided to a language model, including instructions, context, and examples that guide the model's response.

Prompt Engineering

The practice of crafting precise, effective prompts to reliably guide AI systems toward desired outputs.

RAG (Retrieval-Augmented Generation)

An architecture that combines a language model with a document retrieval system, grounding model responses in specific retrieved documents.

Reinforcement Learning from Human Feedback (RLHF)

A training approach in which human raters evaluate model outputs and those ratings are used to fine-tune the model toward preferred responses.

Temperature

A parameter controlling the randomness of AI outputs. Lower temperature produces more deterministic outputs; higher temperature produces more varied outputs.

Token

The basic unit of text that a language model processes. Roughly 3/4 of a word in English.

Transformer

The neural network architecture underlying virtually all modern large language models, introduced in the 2017 paper 'Attention Is All You Need.'

Zero-Shot Prompting

Asking an AI to perform a task without providing examples, relying entirely on the model's pre-trained capabilities.

REFERENCES AND FURTHER READING

FOUNDATIONAL AI HISTORY AND THEORY

1. Turing, A. M. (1950). Computing Machinery and Intelligence. Mind, 59(236), 433-460.
2. McCarthy, J., Minsky, M. L., Rochester, N., & Shannon, C. E. (1955). A Proposal for the Dartmouth Summer Research Project on Artificial Intelligence.
3. Searle, J. R. (1980). Minds, Brains, and Programs. Behavioral and Brain Sciences, 3(3), 417-424.
4. Krizhevsky, A., Sutskever, I., & Hinton, G. E. (2012). ImageNet Classification with Deep Convolutional Neural Networks. NeurIPS 2012.
5. Vaswani, A., Shazeer, N., Parmar, N., et al. (2017). Attention Is All You Need. NeurIPS 2017.

LARGE LANGUAGE MODELS AND CAPABILITIES

6. Brown, T., Mann, B., Ryder, N., et al. (2020). Language Models are Few-Shot Learners. NeurIPS 2020.
7. Wei, J., Wang, X., Schuurmans, D., et al. (2022). Chain-of-Thought Prompting Elicits Reasoning in Large Language Models. NeurIPS 2022.
8. Hu, K. (2023, February 2). ChatGPT sets record for fastest-growing user base. Reuters.
9. Shumailov, I., Shumaylov, Z., Zhao, Y., et al. (2023). The Curse of Recursion: Training on Generated Data Makes Models Forget. arXiv:2305.17493.

10. Epoch AI. (2024). Will we run out of data? Insights from modeling the human data generation process.

ECONOMIC AND WORKFORCE IMPACT

11. Goldman Sachs Economics Research. (2023). The Potentially Large Effects of Artificial Intelligence on Economic Growth.

12. McKinsey Global Institute. (2023). The Economic Potential of Generative AI: The Next Productivity Frontier.

13. World Economic Forum. (2020). The Future of Jobs Report 2020.

14. McKinsey Global Institute. (2024). The State of AI in 2024.

AI SAFETY, ETHICS, AND GOVERNANCE

15. European Parliament. (2024). Regulation (EU) 2024/1689 on Artificial Intelligence (AI Act).

16. Executive Office of the President. (2023). Executive Order 14110: Safe, Secure, and Trustworthy Development and Use of Artificial Intelligence. Federal Register, 88(210), 75191.

17. Liang, W., Yuksekgonul, M., Mao, Y., et al. (2023). GPT detectors are biased against non-native English writers. Patterns, 4(7), 100779.

18. Home Security Heroes. (2023). 2023 State of Deepfakes.

19. Coalition for Content Provenance and Authenticity (C2PA). (2023). C2PA Technical Specification v1.3.

AI APPLICATIONS AND DOMAIN STUDIES

20. Jumper, J., Evans, R., Pritzel, A., et al. (2021). Highly accurate protein structure prediction with AlphaFold. Nature, 596, 583-589.

21. Silver, D., Huang, A., Maddison, C. J., et al. (2016). Mastering the game of Go with deep neural networks and tree search. Nature, 529, 484-489.

22. McKinney, S. M., Sieniek, M., et al. (2020). International evaluation of an AI system for breast cancer screening. Nature, 577, 89-94.

23. Zhavoronkov, A., Ivanenkov, Y. A., et al. (2019). Deep learning enables rapid identification of potent DDR1 kinase inhibitors. Nature Biotechnology, 37, 1038-1040.

24. Gomez-Uribe, C. A., & Hunt, N. (2016). The Netflix Recommender System. ACM Transactions on Management Information Systems, 6(4), 1-19.

LEGAL AND PROFESSIONAL CASES

25. Schwartz v. Mata, No. 22-cv-1461 (S.D.N.Y. June 22, 2023).

26. SAG-AFTRA. (2023). SAG-AFTRA 2023 TV/Theatrical Contract.

27. Stanford Human-Centered AI Institute. (2024). AI Index Report 2024. Stanford University.

28. Hsu, F.-h. (2002). Behind Deep Blue. Princeton University Press.

sALLvit™ AI MANAGER CERTIFICATION PROGRAM

The Certified AI Manager (CAM) Credential

Skills Demonstration | Max 10 Cohort | Employer-Recognized | Starting at $595

This book is the assigned reading for the sALLvit™ Certified AI Manager program. Reading gives you the framework. The course is where that framework meets real conditions, real peers, and a real credential. The CAM is earned through a skills demonstration, not a quiz, and is designed for professionals who want evidence of practitioner-level AI management capability that employers can verify.

THREE TRACKS

EXECUTIVE TRACK	MANAGER TRACK	OPERATOR TRACK
Strategic AI literacy for senior leaders. Focuses on governance, risk, ROI, and how to direct AI-capable teams without needing operational depth.	Full-program track. Covers all frameworks in this book through live exercises, agentic deployments, and the complete skills demonstration pathway to CAM certification.	Hands-on practitioner focus. Emphasizes RTCFCS prompting, DVSA workflow, agentic deployment, and tool selection for professionals who build and run AI workflows daily.

What the Program Delivers

- LIVE RTCFCS PROMPTING LABS: Build and stress-test prompts against real business tasks with real-time facilitator feedback on construction and output quality.
- SIX FAILURE MODES DEMONSTRATIONS: See hallucination, the Pander Problem, the Bell Curve Problem, data collapse, systemic bias, and agent error compounding demonstrated live, including the Pander Problem shown in real time on a deliberately flawed budget plan.
- MULTI-MODEL RED TEAMING PRACTICAL: Complete the full 7-phase Corporate Offsite Practical Lab with arithmetic verification, adversarial audit prompts, and a final executive-ready deliverable.
- AGENT GOVERNANCE WORKSHOP: Design, deploy, and document a real agentic workflow under facilitator supervision using the Agent Design Canvas.
- 12-MONTH ROADMAP WORKBOOK: Build your personal Foundation-to-Leadership roadmap as a concrete deliverable with peer accountability built in.
- CAM SKILLS DEMONSTRATION: Earn the Certified AI Manager credential through a

practitioner assessment, not a multiple-choice test.

- ALUMNI NETWORK: Join a professional community of CAM-certified managers. Max-10 cohort size ensures facilitated debrief is genuine.

TWO FORMATS

1-DAY INTENSIVE

Compressed delivery of the full CAM curriculum. Ideal for professionals who want the credential efficiently. In-person or virtual.

4-DAY PROGRAM

Full-depth delivery across four days. Includes extended lab time, individual coaching sessions, and deeper debrief on case studies. Recommended for maximum skill transfer.

GET IN TOUCH

Email Us

contact.us@sallvit-corp.com

We respond within one business day.

Visit Our Website

https://sallvit-corp.com

Courses, resources, and enrollment.

www.ingramcontent.com/pod-product-compliance
Lightning Source LLC
LaVergne TN
LVHW010648110826
845149LV00014B/2993

9798996337453